Gary Graham

Fly Fishing
Southern Baja

A Quick, Clear Understanding of
How & Where to Fly Fish
Baja's Famous and Remote Saltwaters

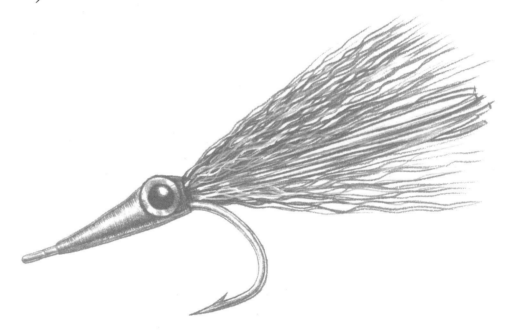

NO NONSENSE

Fly Fishing Southern Baja

© 2004 No Nonsense Fly Fishing Guidebooks
ISBN #1-892469-00-6

Published by:
No Nonsense Fly Fishing Guidebooks
7493 N. Oracle Road Suite 125
Tucson, AZ 85704
(520) 547-2462
www.nononsenseguides.com

Printed in the U.S.A.

Author: Gary Graham

Maps & Illustrations: Pete Chadwell

Cover Design: Pete Chadwell

Editors: David Banks, Jim Yuskavitch, Yvonne Graham

Production & Art Direction: Pete Chadwell

Cover Photos: Verna Benbow, Gene Kira, Glenn Kishi

No Nonsense Guides believes that in addition to local information and gear, fly fishers need clean water and healthy fish. The publisher encourages preservation, improvement, conservation, enjoyment and understanding of our waters and their inhabitants. A good way to do this is to support organizations dedicated to these ideas.

No Nonsense Guides is a member and sponsor of, and donor to The International Game Fish Association, Trout Unlimited, The Federation of Fly Fishers, Oregon Trout, California Trout, New Mexico Trout, American Fly Fishing Trade Association, American Rivers, and Ducks Unlimited. We encourage you to get involved, learn more and to join such organizations. IGFA (954) 941-3474, Trout Unlimited (800) 834-2419 • Federation of Fly Fishers (406) 585-7592 • Oregon Trout (503) 222-9091 • California Trout (415) 392-8887 • New Mexico Trout (505) 344-6363 • A.F.F.T.A. (360) 636-0708 • American Rivers (202) 347-7550 • Ducks Unlimited: (901) 758-3825.

Disclaimer - While this guide will greatly help readers to fly fish, it is not a substitute for caution, good judgment and the services of a qualified guide or outfitter.

Dedication

*T*his book is dedicated to family and friends.
To the love of my life, Yvonne: This book would not have been possible without her love, encouragement, patience and editing skills. To Greg, Geoff, Julie, Mike and Teri, our five children, and Jerry, our son-in-law. To Casey, Elliott, Joshua, Lindsey and Zane, our five grandchildren. Their interest and enthusiasm in my fishing have been a constant source of delight. To my parents, Ed and Lynn Graham who, many years ago, encouraged me to pursue my dreams. To the friends that I have made over the years pursuing these dreams.

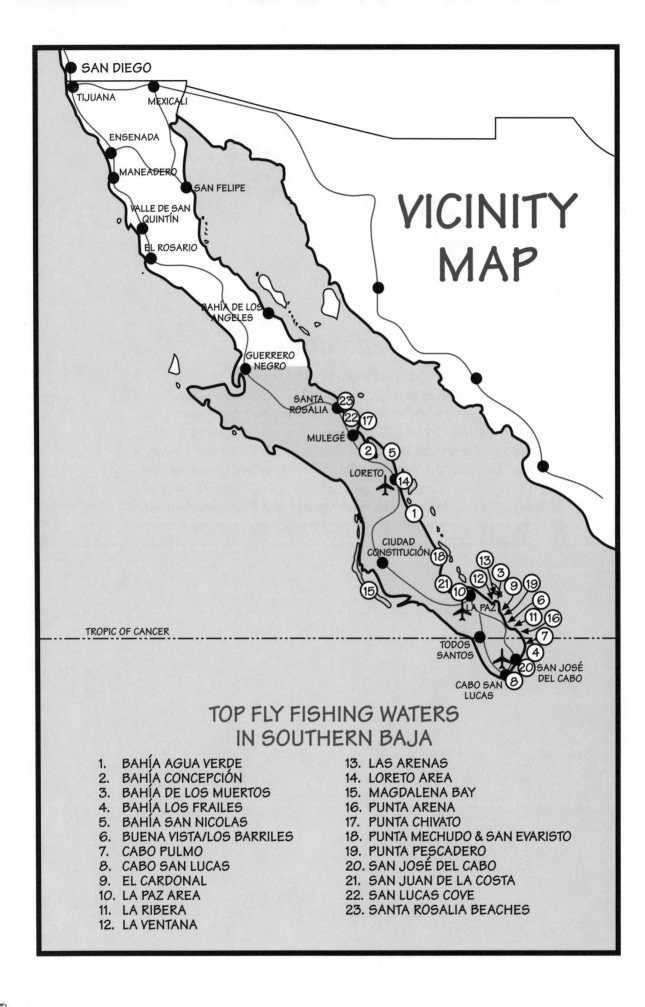

VICINITY MAP

SAN DIEGO
TIJUANA
MEXICALI
ENSENADA
MANEADERO
SAN FELIPE
VALLE DE SAN QUINTÍN
EL ROSARIO
BAHÍA DE LOS ANGELES
GUERRERO NEGRO
SANTA ROSALIA
MULEGÉ
LORETO
CIUDAD CONSTITUCIÓN
LA PAZ
TODOS SANTOS
CABO SAN LUCAS
SAN JOSÉ DEL CABO

TROPIC OF CANCER

TOP FLY FISHING WATERS
IN SOUTHERN BAJA

1. BAHÍA AGUA VERDE
2. BAHÍA CONCEPCIÓN
3. BAHÍA DE LOS MUERTOS
4. BAHÍA LOS FRAILES
5. BAHÍA SAN NICOLAS
6. BUENA VISTA/LOS BARRILES
7. CABO PULMO
8. CABO SAN LUCAS
9. EL CARDONAL
10. LA PAZ AREA
11. LA RIBERA
12. LA VENTANA
13. LAS ARENAS
14. LORETO AREA
15. MAGDALENA BAY
16. PUNTA ARENA
17. PUNTA CHIVATO
18. PUNTA MECHUDO & SAN EVARISTO
19. PUNTA PESCADERO
20. SAN JOSÉ DEL CABO
21. SAN JUAN DE LA COSTA
22. SAN LUCAS COVE
23. SANTA ROSALIA BEACHES

Contents

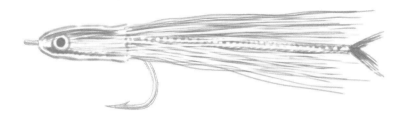

The
No Nonsense Creed

*T*he best way to go fly fishing is to find out a little something about the water, and then just go. Wrong turns, surprises, self-reliance and discovering something new, even in familiar waters, are what make the memories.

The next best way is to learn enough from a local fisherman to save you from going too far wrong. You'll still find the water yourself, and it still feels as if you were the first to discover it.

This is the idea for our unique No Nonsense fly fishing series. Our books reveal little hush-hush information, yet they give all you need to find what will become your own secret places.

Painstakingly pared down, our writing is elegantly simple. Each title offers a local fly fishing expert's candid tour of favorite fly fishing waters. Nothing is oversold or out of proportion. Everything is authentic, especially the discoveries and experiences you get after using our books. In his outstanding book *Jerusalem Creek*, Ted Leeson echoes our idea.

> *"Discovering a new trout stream is a wonderful thing, and even if its where-abouts are common knowledge, to come upon the place yourself for the first time is nonetheless true discovery."*

No Nonsense Fly Fishing Guidebooks give you a quick, clear understanding of the essential information needed to fly fish a region's most outstanding waters. The authors are highly experienced and qualified local fly fishers. Maps are tidy versions of the author's sketches.

Preface

*A*book is a lot like life. It's the sum of the people you've met and your experiences. I want to acknowledge here some people and some experiences that helped me write this guidebook.

My uncle, **Charles Fisher**, took the time to teach me (at age six) how to fish for batrays and stripers in San Francisco Bay. **Jim Melton** and my father, **Ed Graham**, kindled the flame of fishing enthusiasm. **Ray Cannon** brought Baja to my attention. **Tom Miller** kindly let me tag along on his Baja adventures. **Gene Kira** shares his vast knowledge of Baja with me.

Great fishermen of the West Coast have helped me understand the subtleties of the Pacific Ocean and the Sea of Cortez. They include **Gene Grimes, Jack Bohannon, Bruce Kessler, Peter Groesbeck, Steve Lasley** and **Don McAdams.**

Many have fished with me regularly over the last twenty-five years; my wife **Yvonne,** my son **Greg, Don Abrego, Mel Ibey** and **R.C. Newton. Don Sloan** introduced me to fly fishing and never lets me forget it.

Finally, to some of the fly fishing greats who took the time to establish my fly fishing foundation: **Nick Curcione, Jeff Solis, Ed Jaworoski, Mike Wolverton** and **Bob Popovics.**

Introduction

Some background on Southern Baja and fly fishing

*I*n the 16th century, Spanish explorers depicted Baja, not as a peninsula, but an island. This mischaracterization is understandable because there is far more coast to Baja than connection to the continent. The island myth, long dispelled, still seems to fit. Baja's three sides of saltwater translates to over 2,000 miles of coastline. With jagged, rocky coastlines, white sandy beaches and many lagoons, Baja has it all for adventuresome fly fishers. There is even, believe it or not, a trout stream hiding in the foothills of Baja Norte (north). It was stocked sometime around 1904.

After many false starts Baja is now becoming one of the globe's premier destinations for flyrodders. As evidence of this "coming of age" there are now shops specializing in saltwater fly fishing. Just a short twenty years ago these were unheard of. So were hotels, captains and mates who encourage and service enthusiasts of this wonderful style of fishing. Part of the attraction to Baja, and southern Baja in particular, is the fishing conditions that please almost everyone. Whether a beginner or a seasoned pro, few places in the world provide such a variety of fly fishing challenges.

Over thirty years ago people like Harry Kime, Jerry Klink and Tom Miller paved the way for the fly angler in Baja. Now Nick Curcione, Trey Combs, Terry and Wendy Gunn, Ken Hanley, Ed Jaworoski, Bob Popovics, Jeff Solis, Lani Waller and many others continue to promote saltwater fly fishing. As a result of the work of these people, Baja is now flyrod friendly. In almost every major sport fishing center, especially in the southern part of Baja, you can now find someone who is eager to accommodate your fly fishing needs.

My first notions of Baja were newspaper stories I read as an adolescent in Southern California. Large fish and large catches kindled my teenage fantasies of wide open fishing. Then, until the late '60s, I was satisfied to fish the local kelp beds and areas offshore of Southern California. In 1969, with my eight year-old-son Greg in tow, I flew to Ed Tabor's Flying Sportsmen Lodge in Loreto. After that first exposure there was no looking back! Yellowtail, dorado, and roosterfish fed what was to become an insatiable quest for the next fish in the next spot. It didn't matter to me whether I fished from the shore or on a boat, Baja had it and it fascinated me. Since then I have come to realize the other virtues of Baja.

The people, the land, the culture and the history have all added to my enchantment.

Over the last 10 years my fishing evolved from conventional tackle to saltwater-flyrod. Now (finally) I'm in a place in life where I can spend more than two hundred days a year in Baja, most of them with a flyrod in my hand. I also have a little time to record my Baja fly fishing information. It is a pleasure to have this opportunity to pass on to you the places I've found, or have been shown, that will challenge your fly fishing skills and delight your senses in so many ways. Now, on to the background information you'll need to fly fish this fantastic place.

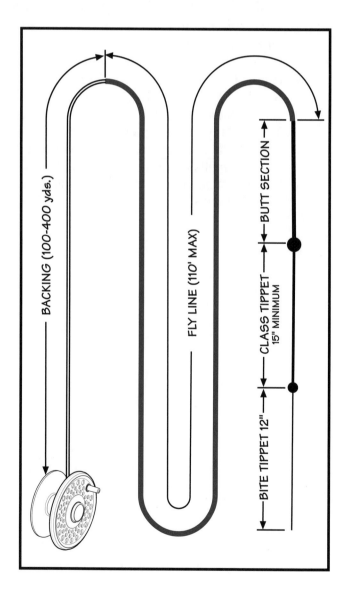

The Southern Baja
No Nonsense Fly-O-Matic

A quick-start guide to basic and unique features of fly fishing in Southern Baja

Gamefish

Marlin, sailfish, tuna, dorado, wahoo, skipjack, yellowtail, jack crevalle, amberjacks, roosterfish, cabrilla, pompano, ladyfish, grouper, white seabass, snook and bonefish are only a few of the reported 850 species found along the shores of Baja that are eager to take a fly.

Catch and Release

Anglers the world over have come to recognize the importance of catch and release and Baja anglers are no different. Most species may be returned to the water with no apparent harm. Certainly billfish, roosterfish and jacks, which have very little food value, should be released if possible. Keeping a potential world record, or occasionally taking a fish for the table probably won't harm the resource.

Weather

Spring and fall are very pleasant in southern Baja, with highs in the 80s and lows in the 60s. Baja may reach 110 degrees during the summer with lows in the 70s. Humidity can be a factor during the late summer months. September is the time to look out for chubascos (hurricanes). During winter months, (November 15th - April 1st) lows are in the mid 50s and high temperatures are in the upper 70s. At this time the entire coast of the Sea of Cortez can also be affected by north winds. Depending on intensity these winds can affect your plans and fly fishing. Check current satellite photos and reliable weather reports (see appendix) when planning your trip.

Pests and Insects

Baja is desert country and has all the critters, good and bad, you would expect in such a region. If you are allergic to any kind of bites check with your doctor and carry any anti-venom you may require. The only poisonous snake in Baja is the rattler, and they are rarely seen. Nonetheless, a snake bite kit is not a bad idea if you are fishing in remote areas. Scorpions are fairly common. Their sting is similar to a bee's. One may also come across bees, wasps, mosquitoes and no-see-ums. A good repellent is usually enough to keep these insects away. While in the water it's a good idea to watch for jellyfish that seem to come and go with the tides. Sometimes they are found dead on the beach at the high tide line (they can still sting). Stingrays can be a nuisance, though they are not found in all areas. Where they are common, shuffle while you walk to scare them away. All the stings noted above can be treated with topical ointments, antihistamine spray or tablets, or both.

Shore

Baja beaches can be sand, rock, gravel or just plain dirt. For our purposes in this guidebook, shore fishing includes kick-boats or float tubes.

Inshore

This area is shoreline out to the first drop-off, or where the water color changes.

Offshore

This starts where there is no discernible color change caused by the bottom. Also called bluewater or deep sea.

Tides

Know these basics for fly fishing from shore and inshore. The gravitational pull of the moon and wind causes tides. Every 14 days tide phases repeat themselves. Typically there are 2 high and 2 low tides a day, each rising or falling in about a 6-hour period. Tides rise or fall about one hour later than they did the day before. These facts are constant if the weather, water depth and wind are constant. A neap tide occurs during quarter moon phases, lasts for 7 days and rises and falls very little. A spring tide occurs during dark and full moon phases, takes place the 7 days after a neap tide and has a greater rise and fall. Baitfish are transported by tides.

Rods

When fly fishing Baja use a rod designed specifically for saltwater. I recommend 3 or 4 piece rods because they're easier for the traveling angler. For Baja beaches a 9', 8 weight rod is adequate.

Inshore, a 10 weight rod will work for most conditions, unless you've hooked a 20-lb. (or larger) fish. Then you may want to go with a 12 weight. Offshore for larger dorado, tuna, and wahoo use the 12 weight. For billfish and tuna bring the 14 weight.

Reels

Choose a reel that approximates the rod weight, noting that not all manufacturers designate sizes to match the rod weight. For the beach and inshore, use only reels that hold 200 to 250 yards of 20-lb. backing. Offshore reels should hold a minimum of 400 yards of 30-lb. backing. All reels should have a disk drag system and be designed for saltwater. Extra spools are a good way to have different systems at the ready.

Lines, Leaders, Backing

Fly lines such as Teeny, Orvis Depth Charge, etc., a shooting head system, or intermediate lines should be your choice for Baja. These lines work well from beach to offshore. Floating lines are OK for fishing poppers or over rock reefs. Tapered leaders are not necessary. Use good quality monofilament or fluorocarbon leader material in sizes from 12 to 20 lb. test. Shock tippets should range from 40 to 60 to 80 lb., and wire is best for the toothy ones. In Baja your backing will be stretched frequently so use high visibility dacron line, 20 to 30 lb. test and make sure it is not old and weak! An extra spool of backing is handy in Baja.

Other Equipment

A waterproof gear bag with built in rod tubes is handy when traveling. Try to find one that is small enough to carry on the plane. Footwear is critical when fishing the shoreline! Sandals, tennis shoes, flats booties or pull on boots (used for diving) are ideal. A stripping basket, either a plastic trash can or a specially designed high tech wonder is helpful. Bring a file, saltwater pliers, clippers, forceps, small scale, camera, film, batteries, sun block, polarized sunglasses and an assortment of barrel and snap swivels.

Saltwater Fly Fishing Hints

Always pre-rig your rod, with the fly hooked on the stripping guide and the leader looped around the reel. When you board the boat or go to the beach to fish you will, invariably, be trying to get your rod out and rigged while fish are boiling and waiting for your cast. Also, always watch the fly all the way to the end of your retrieve. Many times fish follow, without striking, until the fly is removed from the water. If this happens, quickly roll cast and put the fly back in play. Here are other quick, basic hints.

- Change backing often.
- Sharpen hooks frequently.
- Crimp down the barbs on the hooks.
- Don't use leaders longer than 6'.
- Don't strike or set the hook with the rod tip.
- Practice tying knots until you can tie them in the dark.
- Use a two-handed retrieve when stripping your line in.
- Clean your tackle with freshwater at the end of each day.
- Use flies the length of the baitfish on which the fish are feeding.

Saltwater Skills

Baja offers a unique setting to allow you to improve your fly fishing skills. Whether a novice or a seasoned pro, this is the place to practice and improve. You will have opportunities to cast and catch fish, regardless of your casting skills. It's a good idea to practice casting larger flies before you make the trip. If you have the time, take a casting lesson.

Travel Tips To Baja, Mexico

American citizens must bring a valid passport or birth certificate with photo ID, such as a driver's license. You will be issued a Tourist Permit and Customs Declaration on the airplane, or at the border. These must be filled out before your arrival.

Electricity is standard 110 volt so your appliances are usable. Long distance telephone charges are high in Mexico. Most hotels can receive or send faxes for you for a small fee. If driving, exchange currency for Mexican pesos. Most all places take dollars and or travelers checks.

Tips for the skipper and deckhand is usually around $30 U.S. If the crew has done an exceptional job, use your judgment and tip accordingly. As of this writing, in most places bait should cost about $20.

Most cellular phones work in Baja. Check with your service provider before leaving for your trip.

Best Months to Fly Fish Southern Baja by Region

SANTA ROSALIA & SAN LUCAS COVE
SITES 22 & 23

FISH	JAN	FEB	MAR	APR	MAY	JUN	JULY	AUG	SEPT	OCT	NOV	DEC
SIERRA												
ROOSTERFISH												
LADYFISH												
CORVINA												
GROUPER												
SPOTTED BAY BASS												
CABRILLA												
SKIPJACK												
YELLOWTAIL												
DORADO												
STRIPED MARLIN												
TUNA												

■ EXCELLENT   ■ FAIR   ☐ POOR

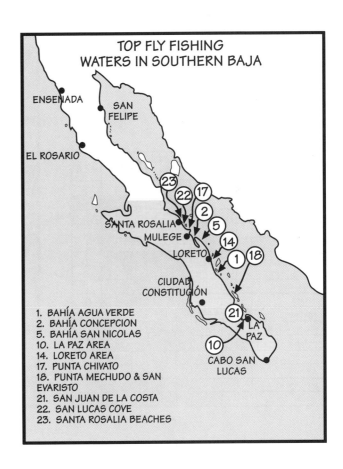

TOP FLY FISHING WATERS IN SOUTHERN BAJA

ENSENADA
SAN FELIPE
EL ROSARIO
23
22
17
2
5
SANTA ROSALIA
MULEGE
14
18
LORETO
1
CIUDAD CONSTITUCIÓN
21
LA PAZ
10
CABO SAN LUCAS

1. BAHÍA AGUA VERDE
2. BAHÍA CONCEPCION
5. BAHÍA SAN NICOLAS
10. LA PAZ AREA
14. LORETO AREA
17. PUNTA CHIVATO
18. PUNTA MECHUDO & SAN EVARISTO
21. SAN JUAN DE LA COSTA
22. SAN LUCAS COVE
23. SANTA ROSALIA BEACHES

BAHÍA CONCEPCIÓN, BAHÍA SAN NICOLAS & PUNTA CHIVATO
SITES 2, 5 & 17

FISH	JAN	FEB	MAR	APR	MAY	JUN	JULY	AUG	SEPT	OCT	NOV	DEC
SIERRA												
PARGO												
GROUPER												
CABRILLA												
NEEDLEFISH												
LADYFISH												
YELLOWTAIL												
SKIPJACK												
DORADO												
STRIPED MARLIN												
TUNA												
SAILFISH												

BAHÍA AGUA VERDE & LORETO AREA
SITES 1 & 14

FISH	JAN	FEB	MAR	APR	MAY	JUN	JULY	AUG	SEPT	OCT	NOV	DEC
SIERRA												
ROOSTERFISH												
JACKS												
PARGO												
GROUPER												
CABRILLA												
SKIPJACK												
NEEDLEFISH												
YELLOWTAIL												
DORADO												
SAILFISH												
STRIPED MARLIN												

LA PAZ AREA, SAN JUAN DE LA COSTA, PUNTA MECHUDO & SAN EVARISTO
SITES 10, 21 & 18

FISH	JAN	FEB	MAR	APR	MAY	JUN	JULY	AUG	SEPT	OCT	NOV	DEC
SIERRA												
ROOSTERFISH												
PARGO												
NEEDLEFISH												
GROUPER												
CABRILLA												
SKIPJACK												
DORADO												
YELLOWTAIL												
STRIPED MARLIN												
TUNA												
SAILFISH												

Best Months to Fly Fish Southern Baja by Region

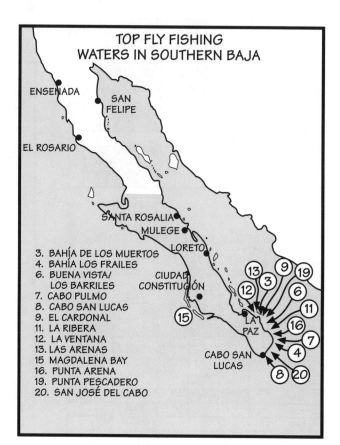

TOP FLY FISHING WATERS IN SOUTHERN BAJA

3. BAHÍA DE LOS MUERTOS
4. BAHÍA LOS FRAILES
6. BUENA VISTA/LOS BARRILES
7. CABO PULMO
8. CABO SAN LUCAS
9. EL CARDONAL
11. LA RIBERA
12. LA VENTANA
13. LAS ARENAS
15. MAGDALENA BAY
16. PUNTA ARENA
19. PUNTA PESCADERO
20. SAN JOSÉ DEL CABO

EAST CAPE AREA
SITES 3,4,6,7,9,11,12,13,16 & 19

FISH	JAN	FEB	MAR	APR	MAY	JUN	JULY	AUG	SEPT	OCT	NOV	DEC
SIERRA												
ROOSTERFISH												
PARGO												
GROUPER												
CABRILLA												
JACKS												
LADYFISH												
NEEDLEFISH												
DORADO												
YELLOWTAIL												
STRIPED MARLIN												
SKIPJACK												
TUNA												
SAILFISH												
BLUE MARLIN												
WAHOO												

MAGDALENA BAY
SITE 15

FISH	JAN	FEB	MAR	APR	MAY	JUN	JULY	AUG	SEPT	OCT	NOV	DEC
SIERRA												
CORVINA												
PARGO												
GROUPER												
SPOTTED BAY BASS												
HALIBUT												
POMPANO												
SNOOK												
DORADO												
STRIPED MARLIN												
TUNA												
WAHOO												

CABO SAN LUCAS AND SAN JOSÉ DEL CABO,
SITES 8 & 20

FISH	JAN	FEB	MAR	APR	MAY	JUN	JULY	AUG	SEPT	OCT	NOV	DEC
SIERRA												
ROOSTERFISH												
JACKS												
PARGO												
GROUPER												
CABRILLA												
SKIPJACK												
DORADO												
STRIPED MARLIN												
TUNA												
SAILFISH												
BLUE MARLIN												
WAHOO												

A No Nonsense Display of
Common Gamefish in Southern Baja

LADYFISH
(**Sab-A-lo**) 1 - 6 lbs. Silvery body, acrobatic fighter, sometimes referred to as "poor man's tarpon." Streamers, Clousers allowed to sink will attract any fish in the area. If not bitten use fast retrieve. With poppers use a slow steady retrieve.

CABRILLA
(**Cah-BREE-yah**) 1 - 10 lbs. Variety of colors and sub species. Usually found around rock structure. Sometimes seen cruising the sandy beaches looking for food. Clouser ideal fly for this scrapper. Use a slower retrieve and allow the fly to bounce along the sand or rocks.

NEEDLEFISH
(**Mar-see-AHL**) 2 - 15 lbs. Bluish green above, silvery below. Good fighter, will bite almost any fly presented. Very difficult to hook because of bony mouth.

MEXICAN LOOKDOWN
(**Cho-PET-Ah**) 1 - 3 lbs. Inshore, beach. Bluish green back, silver sides. Often caught when targeting other species. Fair fighter.

CORNETFISH
(**Cor-NET-a**) 1 - 3 lbs. Beach and inshore. Brownish above, lighter underneath, fair fighter that sometimes swims backwards. Probably most common fish caught on a fly in Baja. If caught, you're probably retrieving the fly too slowly.

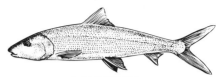

BONEFISH
(**Lisa**) 1 - 3 lbs. Brownish Silver above, white underneath. Common in shallow lagoons and estuaries. Fair fighter. Taken on shrimp and crab patterns.

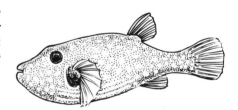

PUFFER FISH
(**Bo-le-te**) 1 - 3 lbs. Inshore and beach. Brown body. Puffs up like a balloon when hooked. Poor fighter is incidental catch that requires forceps to remove fly.

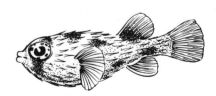

PORCUPINE FISH
(**Pez eh-ri-so**) 1 - 3 lbs. Tan body, long sharp spines. Puffs up like a balloon when hooked. Poor fighter. Dead ones on the beach are hard on bare feet!

15

A No Nonsense Display of
Common Gamefish in Southern Baja

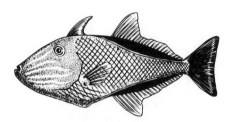

TRIGGERFISH
(Co-chi) *1 - 5 lbs. Inshore, beach. Brownish body, toothy. Tears streamers and Clouser apart. Stubborn fighter, bring lots of flies.*

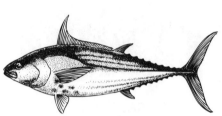

BLACK SKIPJACK
(Bah-ree-leh-teh) *3 - 16 lbs. Inshore, dark blue back, silver sides, dark stripes, 3 or 4 black spots on belly. Use streamers, Clousers and poppers. Strip-strike to set hook. Strong fast fighter, stays around boat.*

GAFFTOPSAIL POMPANO
(Pah-lo-MAY-tah) *1 - 5 lbs. Silver gray, yellow to bronze fins. Often in surf line. Well-cast Clouser or streamer gets attention. If bigger, you probably wouldn't land one.*

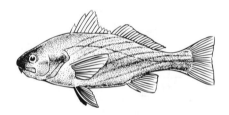

YELLOWFIN CROAKER
(Ron-ca-dor) *1 - 4 lbs. Onshore and beach. Grayish with brown-black wavy lines on side, fins yellowish. Clousers and streamers lure spirited fighter to come out.*

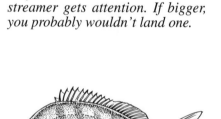

PACIFIC PORGY
(Mo-Ha-dah) *1 - 5 lbs. Reddish-green back, silver to gray sides with dark bars. Crab patterns for these fair fighters in surf line.*

SIERRA
(See-AIR-ah) *1 - 10 lbs. Inshore and beach. Dark blue back, sides silvery with yellowish spots. Good fighter with sharp teeth. Streamers and poppers with a 6" wire shock tippet are the ticket. A fast retrieve gets hard strikes and lightning runs that will amaze.*

BARRED PARGO
(PAR-go) *3 - 20 lbs. Inshore, beach. Called mutton snapper on U.S. East Coast. Greenish bronze back, reddish sides, dark bars. Strong fighter. Sight cast in rocks or along sandy beach with Clouser.*

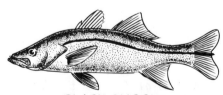

BLACK SNOOK
(Roh-BAH-lo) *2 - 40 lbs. Inshore, beaches with dirty water, lagoons. Bluish back, silver sides, black lateral line. Streamers, poppers best attractors for these strong fighters.*

A No Nonsense Display of
Common Gamefish in Southern Baja

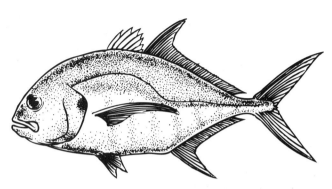

JACK CREVALLE
(TOR-o) *2 - 50 lbs. Inshore, beach. Silver gray, black spots on gill cover and pectoral fin. When feeding will take most any fly. Poppers, streamers or Clousers cast into a school of Toro feeding on sardina produce hard strikes. Rough and tumble fighters.*

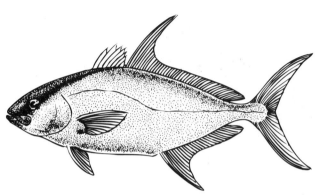

PACIFIC AMBERJACK
(Pez FUER-tay) *5 - 80 lbs. Inshore and beach. Bronze back with cream to yellow belly. Streamers and Clousers retrieved quickly entice these strong fish.*

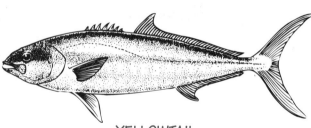

YELLOWTAIL
(Who-REL) *5 - 60 lbs. Inshore, beach. Blue-gray to olive back, yellow stripe on silver sides, yellow tail. Caught on surface or deep. Use fully extended shooting head, weighted streamer or Clouser for deep. Very strong, quick, hard fighter, challenges you and your tackle.*

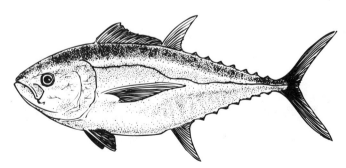

YELLOWFIN TUNA
(A-tun) *15 - 100 lbs. Dark blue back, silver sides, yellow fins. For big fish use 60 lb. shock tippet. Streamers, Clousers for these powerful, durable fighters.*

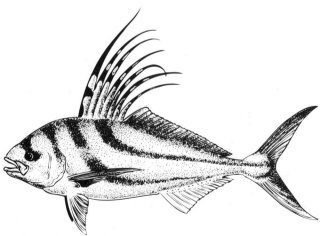

ROOSTERFISH
(Pez GAH-yoh) *1 - 80 lbs. Inshore, beach, occasionally offshore. Dark gray back, silver sides, pronounced diagonal stripes, comblike dorsal fin. Often swims close to shoreline. Various size and color streamers, Clousers, poppers. Not one fly works all the time. Called the permit of Baja. Tough to fool, tough to land.*

A No Nonsense Display of
Common Gamefish in Southern Baja

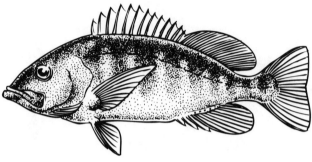

BARRACUDA

(*A-gu-jon*) *Up to 4 feet long and 18 lbs. Found inshore around reefs, piers and sandy flats, or wherever smaller fish congregate. Mexican barracuda are somewhat smaller and have roughly 20 dark vertical bars on the sides.*

DOG SNAPPER

(*PAR-go*) *2 - 50 lbs. Inshore, beach. Reddish body, darker bars, large canine-like teeth. Use wire shock tippet, streamer or Clouser. Determined fighter will quickly cut you off in the rocks.*

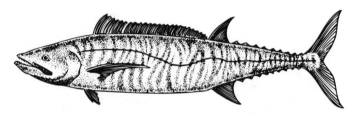

WAHOO

(*Wa-Hoo*) *15 - 100 lbs. Inshore and offshore. Dark blue back fading to silver with iridescent horizontal dark blue bars when excited. Sharp teeth, use a wire shock tippet. Cast large streamers beyond chum line, allow to sink. Produces most spectacular strikes you've ever had. One of the fastest fish in Baja.*

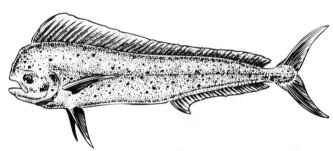

DORADO

(*Doh-RAH-doh*) *2 - 70 lbs. Offshore, inshore, occasionally close enough to shore to get a cast. Changes colors from blue to green on back sides. Yellow with blue and green spots. Great flyrod fish, acrobatics will dazzle. Streamers, poppers, Clousers work well. If chumming, cast beyond chum line, let fly sink until fish feeds on chum, then retrieve fly quickly at constant speed. If fish follows but does not take, immediately cast fly behind fish. After fish turns back to fly, pick fly up, cast back out and let fly sink. Often dorado eat the fly as it sinks. Teasing sometimes works when there's too much bait in water.*

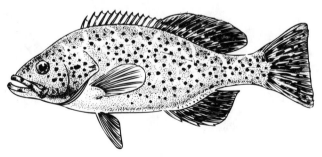

LEOPARD GROUPER

(*Gar-ro-pa*) *Reaches 3 feet and 40 pounds in size. Found in shallow water areas. Identified by small reddish-brown spots over larger, paler splotches.*

Common Billfish in Southern Baja

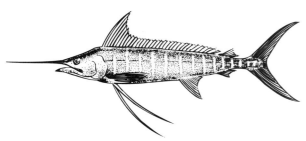

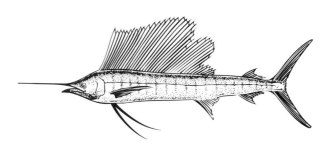

STRIPED MARLIN

(MAHR-leen) *50 - 200 lbs. Offshore. Purple-brown back with light blue bars, silver gray sides, strong acrobatic opponent. Use large streamers and El Tonto with 100 lb. shock tippet and trailing hook. Teased to the boat with live bait or hookless artificials where angler casts fly.*

SAILFISH

(Pez veh-la) *50 - 150 lbs. Offshore, purple-blue back with silver sides. Great flyrod fish, very acrobatic. Use large streamers and El Tonto with trailing hooks and 100 lb. shock tippet. Teased to the boat with live bait or hookless artificials so angler can make fly presentation.*

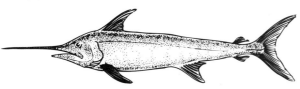

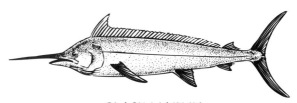

SWORDFISH

(Pez es-pah-dah) *125 - 350 lbs. Offshore, blue back, gray sides and flat bill. The ultimate tough guy that seldom jumps and pulls like a semi-truck.*

BLACK MARLIN

(MAHR-leen nay-groh) *175 - 800 lbs. Offshore, dark blue back with silver sides and no bars, very strong, enduring fighter. Use large streamers and El Tonto with 100 lb. shock tippet and trailing hook. Most frequently teased to the boat for fly caster, like other marlin.*

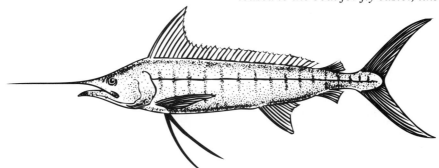

BLUE MARLIN

(MAHR-leen ah-zuhl) *150 - 1,000 lbs. Offshore, dark blue back with silver sides with dark bars, very fast, does little jumping. Use large streamers and El Tonto with 100 lb. shock tippet and trailing hook. Teased to the boat for fly caster, like other marlin.*

The Best Flies to Use in Southern Baja

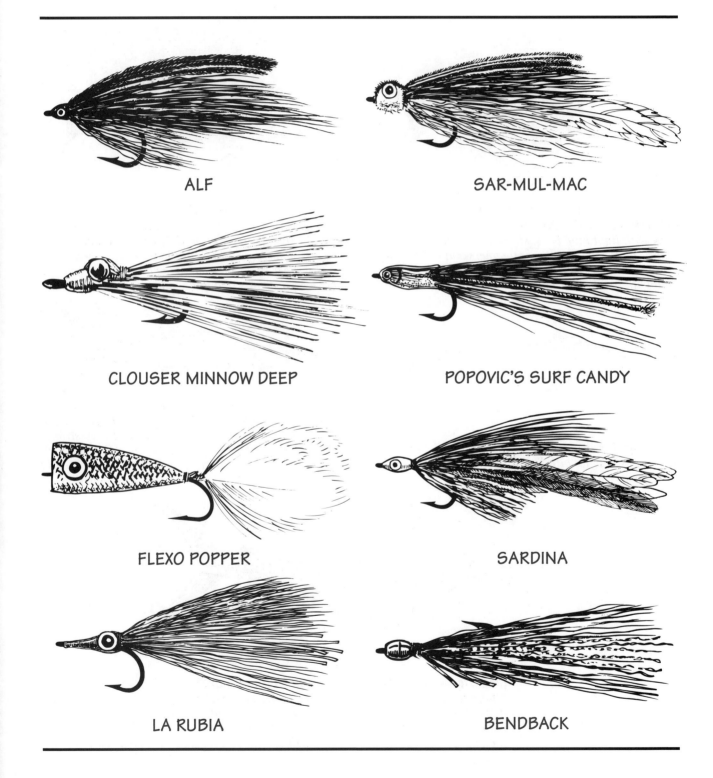

ALF

SAR-MUL-MAC

CLOUSER MINNOW DEEP

POPOVIC'S SURF CANDY

FLEXO POPPER

SARDINA

LA RUBIA

BENDBACK

The Best Flies to Use in Southern Baja

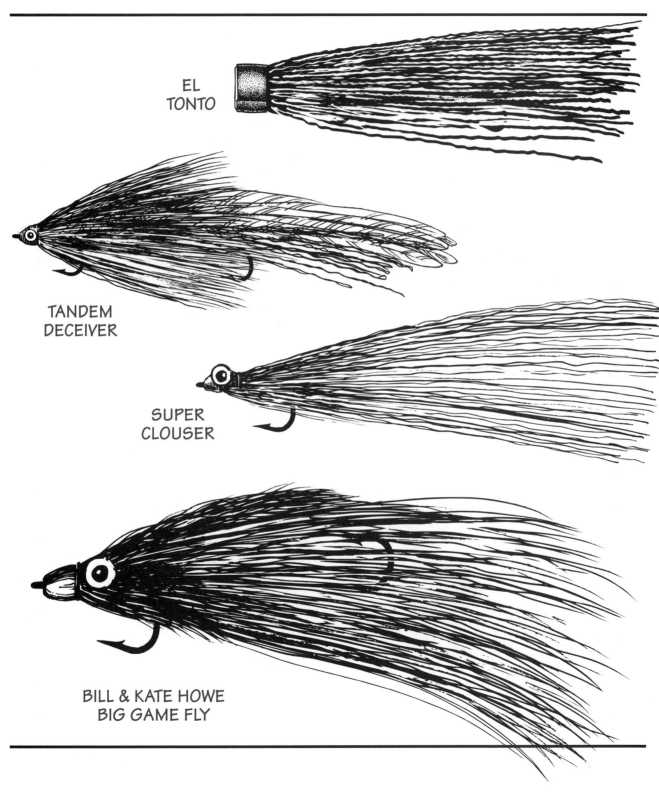

EL
TONTO

TANDEM
DECEIVER

SUPER
CLOUSER

BILL & KATE HOWE
BIG GAME FLY

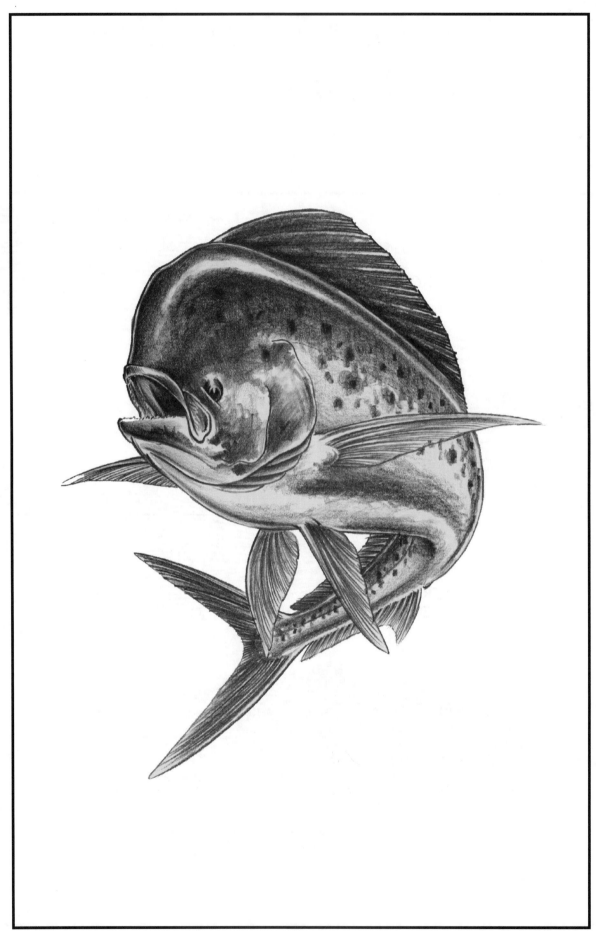

Dorado

Top Southern Baja
Fly Fishing Waters

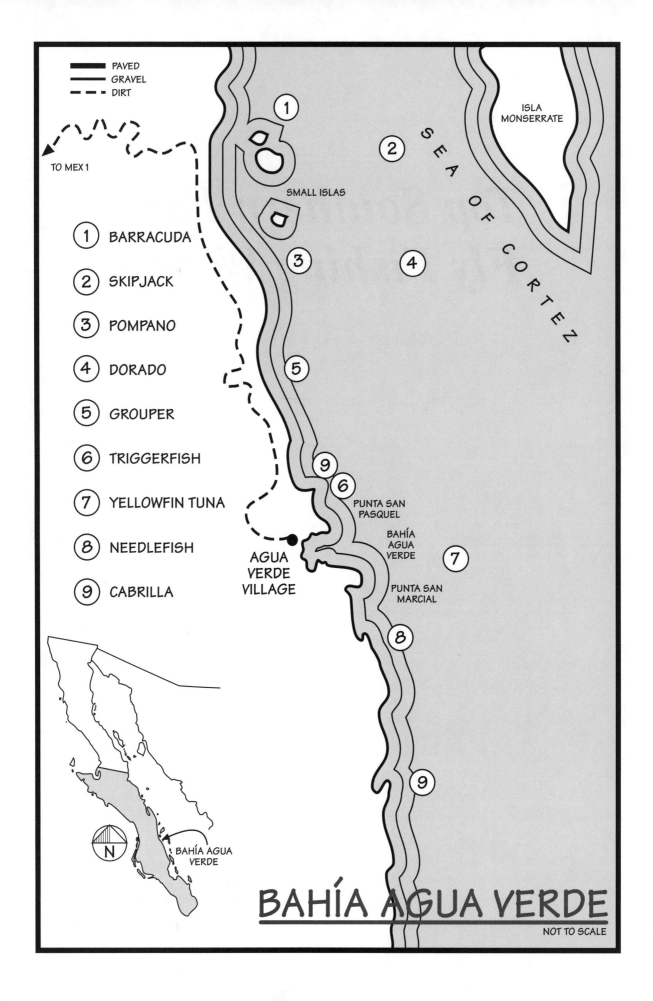

PAVED
GRAVEL
DIRT

TO MEX 1

① BARRACUDA

② SKIPJACK

③ POMPANO

④ DORADO

⑤ GROUPER

⑥ TRIGGERFISH

⑦ YELLOWFIN TUNA

⑧ NEEDLEFISH

⑨ CABRILLA

ISLA MONSERRATE

SEA OF CORTEZ

SMALL ISLAS

PUNTA SAN PASQUEL

BAHÍA AGUA VERDE

PUNTA SAN MARCIAL

AGUA VERDE VILLAGE

N

BAHÍA AGUA VERDE

BAHÍA AGUA VERDE

NOT TO SCALE

Bahía Agua Verde

Agua Verde is the reputed model for the village described in Gene Kira's popular novel, *King of the Moon*. See the appendix for information about this great story of early Baja pangueros.

This area has rocky and sandy shoreline that provides cover for a variety of fish species including cabrilla, triggerfish, rooster, sierra, barracuda, pargo and pompano. A few miles offshore, you'll find dorado, skipjack and yellowfin tuna.

Around the rocks, where cabrilla and pargo often feed, try using small brown, gray or blue Clouser-style flies. Fish both sides of the rocks. Over the sandy areas, use bigger patterns in light blue, gray or green. These flies should mimic sardina and ballyhoo, common baitfish in this area.

The access road leading to the village is approximately 35 miles (56 km) south of Loreto, off Mexico Highway 1. Ascend into the Sierra de la Giganta mountains on a winding, steep section of Mexico 1. Look for a dirt road, off to the east, with a sign for Agua Verde. These 25 miles of well traveled "washboard" road take you to the village.

The first 10 miles (16 km) of this road are a snap. Then you slowly climb a 1,200' summit, and descend 4 miles to the sea on a two vehicle wide road. Some switchbacks have barely enough room for one auto. There are access roads to the shore for the next 10 miles. With the exception of two more points, the next 15 miles (24 km) beyond this stretch is straight and flat.

There is a small fleet of commercial fishing pangas in Agua Verde. You may be able to hire a pangero to take you out in his skiff. For fun, ask for "Chino" or "Abundio."

Types of Fish
Shore: Rock areas - cabrilla, grouper, triggerfish, pompano and croaker. Sand areas - jacks, rooster, pompano, ladyfish, giant needlefish, sierra, pargo, corvina.
Inshore: Dorado, rooster, bonito, sierra, jacks, barracuda, triggerfish, cornet fish, needlefish.
Offshore: Dorado, skipjack and yellowfin tuna.

Equipment to Use - Shore
Rods: 7 to 10 weight, 9'.
Line: Sandy areas - full fly line (350 grain) or shooting head. Rock areas - intermediate or floating with sink-tip.
Leaders: 20 lb., non-tapered mono, 6'.
Reels: Direct or anti-reverse model designed for saltwater with disc drag system and quick take-apart for cleaning.
Other: Polarized sunglasses, stripping basket, foot protection from rocks. Float tube or small inflatable pontoon boat.

Equipment to Use - Inshore
Rods: 8 to 11 weight, 9'.
Line: Full fly line (450 grain), shooting head system or intermediate line to match rod size.
Leaders: 20 lb., non-taper monofilament, 6'. Use short wire shock tippet for sierra.
Reels: Same type as used from shore.
Other: Polarized sunglasses, float tube or small inflatable pontoon boat.

Equipment to Use - Offshore
Rods: 10 to 14 weight, 8' to 9'.
Line: Full fly line (650 grain), shooting head system or intermediate line to match rod size.
Leaders: 20 lb. with shock tippet for billfish.
Reels: Same type as used from shore.
Other: Polarized sunglasses, butt plate for fighting big ones.

Flies to Use
Shore: Hook size 2/0 to 4/0, 1" to 4". Alfs, Clousers, Bendbacks, Deceivers in white, gray, brown, blue and green, sardina and smelt patterns. Tie on lots of flash. Blue, green, or white Popovics Surf Candy.
Inshore: Same as for shore.
Offshore: Large Alf, Clouser and streamers. For billfish, use Tandem Deceivers, Bill & Kate Howe Big Game Fly, El Tonto.

When to Fish
Shore: Low light, morning & afternoon. Incoming tides produce best action. Sight cast midday.
Inshore: Early morning, late afternoon.
Offshore: All day can be good. At slack tide fish where you've seen the most fish that day.

Accommodations & Services
There are no services available in this area, so bring everything you need. Camping is the only overnight option here and is possible anywhere along the beach or in the village of Agua Verde. Return to Loreto for markets, hotels and the closest gas station.

Rating
This area rates a basic 5 for shore, inshore and offshore fly fishing.

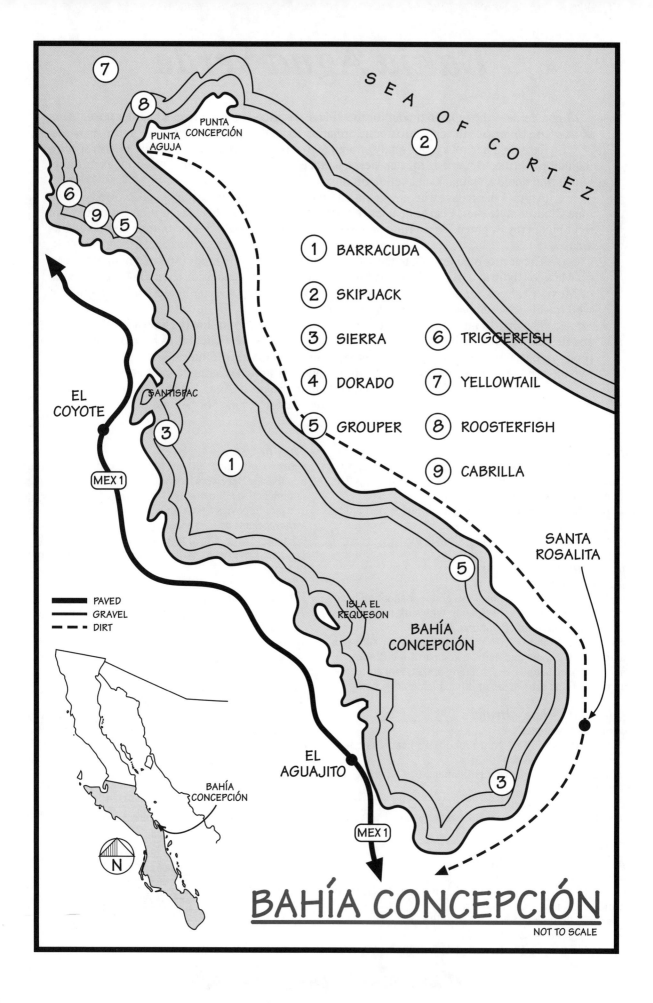

SEA OF CORTEZ

⑦
⑧
PUNTA CONCEPCIÓN
PUNTA AGUJA

②

⑥
⑨ ⑤

① BARRACUDA

② SKIPJACK

③ SIERRA   ⑥ TRIGGERFISH

④ DORADO   ⑦ YELLOWTAIL

⑤ GROUPER   ⑧ ROOSTERFISH

         ⑨ CABRILLA

EL COYOTE
SANTISPAC
③
MEX 1
①

SANTA ROSALITA

⑤

ISLA EL REQUESON
BAHÍA CONCEPCIÓN

PAVED
GRAVEL
DIRT

BAHÍA CONCEPCIÓN

EL AGUAJITO
MEX 1

③

N

BAHÍA CONCEPCIÓN

NOT TO SCALE

Bahía Concepción

*T*hirty miles long, four miles wide and surrounded by land on three sides, Bahía Concepción is one of the most picturesque spots in Baja. Look for yellowtail and barracuda near the north-facing entrance (along with a variety of resident fish) and some sierra and barracuda in the southern reaches of the bay.

For offshore, day trip fly fishing you can charter pangas or cruisers in Mulege. Dorado, sailfish, marlin, skipjack, yellowtail and yellowfin tuna are sometimes found offshore. Commercial fisherman and divers, however, have pretty well picked over this entire area.

An alternative to this is to fish from shore and cast small brown, gray or blue Clousers near the rocks. Look for feeding cabrilla and pargo that are often among these rocks. On the sandy bottom areas use bigger light blue, gray or green patterns, up to 5", to mimic the area's sardina and ballyhoo baitfish.

Access to Bahía Concepción is just a few miles south of Mulege on Mexico 1. With the exception of a 10 mile (16 km) stretch between Bahía Coyote and El Requesón, the entire western shoreline is accessible from Mexico 1. This is a great area for diving, snorkeling, water-skiing and kayaking. Equipment for these activities can be rented in the area.

Types of Fish
Shore: Cabrilla, grouper, triggerfish, pompano, croaker, ladyfish, giant needlefish, sierra and pargo.
Inshore: Dorado, rooster, bonito, sierra, jacks, barracuda, triggerfish, cornet fish and needlefish.
Offshore: Dorado, sailfish, marlin, skipjack, yellowtail and yellowfin tuna.

Equipment to Use - Shore
Rods: 7 to 10 weight, 9'.
Line: Sandy areas, full fly line (350 grain) or shooting head. Rocks, intermediate or floating with sink-tip.
Leaders: 20 lb., non-tapered mono, 6'.
Reels: Direct or anti-reverse model designed for saltwater use with disc drag system and quick take-apart feature for cleaning.
Other: Polarized sunglasses, stripping basket, foot protection from rocks. Float tube or small inflatable pontoon boat. No-seeums and mosquitoes can be a problem in this area, so bring bug repellent.

Equipment to Use - Inshore
Rods: 8 to 11 weight, 9'.
Line: Full fly line (450 grain), shooting head system or intermediate.
Leaders: 20 lb., non-tapered mono, 6'. Use short wire shock tippet for sierra.
Reels: Same type as used from shore.
Other: Polarized sunglasses, float tube or small inflatable pontoon boat.

Equipment to Use - Offshore
Rods: 10 to 12 weight, 8' to 9'. If you try for billfish bring a 14 weight with a good quality reel with lots of backing. If you are not interested in I.G.F.A. rules, try using a 125 lb., 36" bite tippet.

Line: Full fly line (650 grain), shooting head system or intermediate.
Leaders: 20 lb., add shock tippet for billfish.
Reels: Same saltwater system as for inshore only larger.
Other: Polarized sunglasses, butt plate for fighting big fish.

Flies to Use
Shore: Hook size 2/0 to 4/0, 1"- 4". Alf, Clouser, Bendback, Deceivers in white, gray, brown, blue or green, sardina, smelt. Use plenty of flash. Blue, green, or white Popovics Surf Candy.
Inshore: Same flies as from shore (above).
Offshore: 4/0 - 6/0 hook, 4" - 10" Alf, Clouser, streamers, Tandem Deceivers, Bill & Kate Howe Big Game Fly and El Tonto for billfish.

When to Fish
Shore: Low light a.m. and p.m. Incoming tides produce best action. Sight cast midday.
Inshore: Early morning, late afternoon.
Offshore: All day can be good. At slack tide go where you've seen the most fish that day.

Accommodations & Services
Lodgings range from hotels to beach camping to cabanas, bed & breakfasts and even a hostel. Gasoline and all other services are available in Mulege.

Rating
Shore and inshore are a 3. Offshore, a 5.

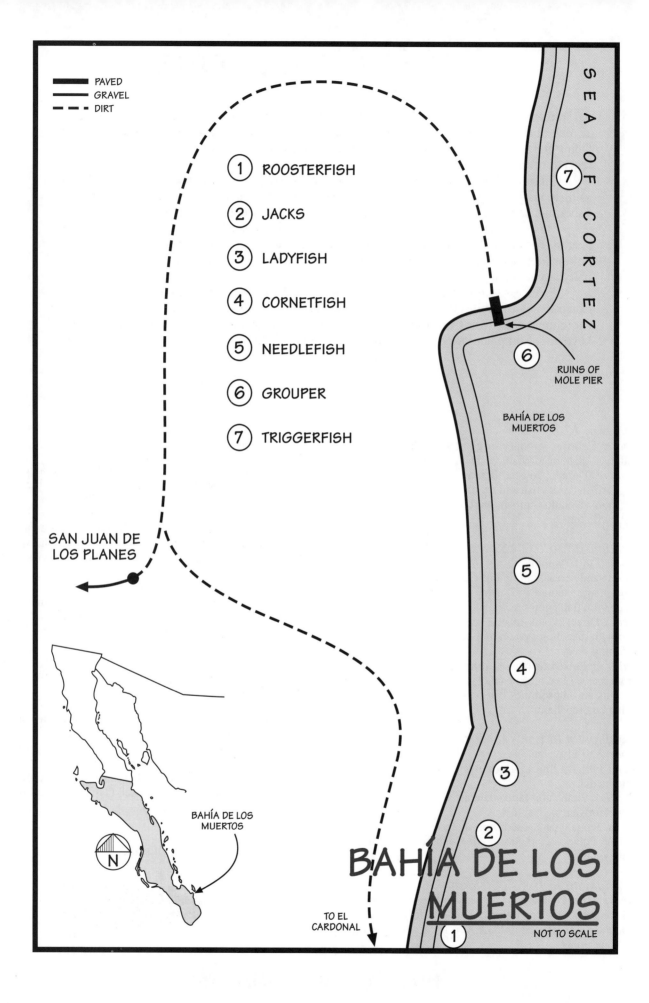

PAVED
GRAVEL
DIRT

1 ROOSTERFISH

2 JACKS

3 LADYFISH

4 CORNETFISH

5 NEEDLEFISH

6 GROUPER

7 TRIGGERFISH

SEA OF CORTEZ

7

6

RUINS OF
MOLE PIER

BAHÍA DE LOS
MUERTOS

SAN JUAN DE
LOS PLANES

5

4

BAHÍA DE LOS
MUERTOS

N

3

2

BAHÍA DE LOS
MUERTOS

TO EL
CARDONAL

1

NOT TO SCALE

Bahía de los Muertos

*T*his bay is a popular anchorage for yachts and sailboats sailing around Baja. Facing east, the bay is well protected from north winds that can cause problems for fly anglers. At the north end of the bay are the ruins of a mole pier, built in the 1920s to accommodate shipment of iron ore from the area. From this vantage point, you can look down into the clear water and see which species are lurking in the rocks or near the surface. It's fun to see what might be waiting for your well-presented fly.

When you have tired of this sport, walk about 500 yards to the south. Here you are on a sandy beach where rooster, jacks, pargo, ladyfish and who knows what else, are patrolling and looking for a free meal. These fish are within easy casting distance which is the main reason you made the long drive to this beautiful bay.

Just a few miles outside the bay, the depth of the Sea of Cortez drops quickly to over 1,000'. This area is sometimes called Gamefish Alley because of all the fish that migrate up into the gulf in the spring and return through the area in the fall.

The drive to this bay can start by following Mexico 1 toward Los Cabos. South of La Paz at km 211, State Highway BCS 286 begins. Follow this road, traveling southeast for some 26 miles (43 km) to the agricultural center of San Juan de los Planes. This road takes you over the 2,500' Sierra de la Laguna mountains and provides a breathtaking view of the azure blue, Bahía de la Ventana with a backdrop of Isla Cerralvo. Continue approximately 13 miles (21 km) east of Los Planes on a graded road to Los Muertos.

Types of Fish
Shore: Sandy beach to the south, rooster, jacks, ladyfish, giant needlefish, pompano and sierra. The rocky point at the north end yields cabrilla, grouper, pargo and triggerfish.
Inshore: Dorado, rooster, bonita, skipjack, sierra, jacks, pompano, triggerfish and giant needlefish. These species crash on baitballs of sardina.
Offshore: Marlin, sailfish, tuna, wahoo and dorado travel through this area.

Equipment to Use - Shore
Rods: 7 to 10 weight, 9'.
Line: Intermediate or floating with sink-tip for rocks. Intermediate can be used on sandy beach areas.
Leaders: 20 lb., non-tapered mono, 6'.
Reels: Direct or anti-reverse, disc drag, designed for saltwater with a quick take-apart feature for cleaning.
Other: Polarized sunglasses, stripping basket, foot protection from the rocks. Float tube or pontoon boat.

Equipment to Use - Inshore
Rods: 8 to 11 weight, 9'.
Line: Full fly line, (450 grain) shooting head/intermediate.
Leaders: 20 lb., non-tapered mono, 6'. Short wire shock tippet for sierra.
Reels: Same as for shore.
Other: Polarized sunglasses, float tube or small pontoon boat.

Equipment to Use - Offshore
Rods: 10 to 14 Weight, 8' - 9'.
Line: Full fly line, (650 grain) shooting head/intermediate.
Leaders: 20 lb. with shock tippet for billfish.
Reels: Same as for other areas only larger.
Other: Polarized sunglasses, butt plate for fighting big ones.

Flies to Use
Shore: Hook size 2/0 to 4/0, 1" - 4", Clouser, Deceiver, Alf, in white, gray, brown, blues or green, sardina and smelt patterns. Use plenty of flash. Popovics Surf Candy in blue, green and white, sand eels in baitfish colors.
Inshore: Same as for shore.
Offshore: Same as above, plus heavy Clousers (hook size 7). For billfish, Tandem Deceivers, Bill & Kate Howe Big Game Fly, El Tonto.

When to Fish
Shore & inshore: Summers are hot, both the fishing and the temperature. Spring and fall are favored because of the cooler weather. Don't dismiss winter. This area has good protection from the north wind and can provide some excellent fishing.
Offshore: This is a year-round fishery, but April - August and October - November 15th is best.

Accommodations & Services
La Paz offers all services and sleeping arrangements from camp grounds to five-star hotels. Las Arenas, a few miles from the area, has full service lodging and meals. Camping available, though much of the property surrounding the bay is private property. Los Planes has limited services.

Rating
Summer and fall rate an 8, winter is a 6.

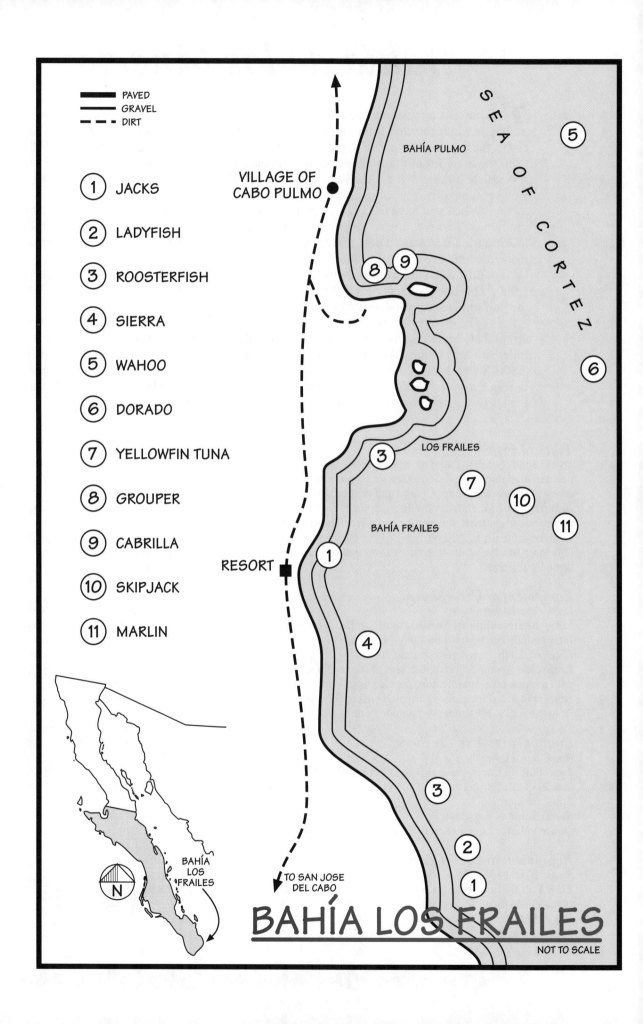

PAVED
GRAVEL
DIRT

1 JACKS

2 LADYFISH

3 ROOSTERFISH

4 SIERRA

5 WAHOO

6 DORADO

7 YELLOWFIN TUNA

8 GROUPER

9 CABRILLA

10 SKIPJACK

11 MARLIN

SEA OF CORTEZ

BAHÍA PULMO

VILLAGE OF CABO PULMO

LOS FRAILES

BAHÍA FRAILES

RESORT

TO SAN JOSE DEL CABO

BAHÍA LOS FRAILES

NOT TO SCALE

BAHÍA LOS FRAILES

N

30

Bahía Los Frailes

Stories of huge tuna and amberjacks caught inside Bahía Los Frailes have drawn conventional anglers here from around the world. This unique bay, a favorite anchorage of yachters cruising the Sea of Cortez, drops off to a 1,000' depth. Along this drop-off are dorado, wahoo, bonita, sierra and other species. The bigger marlin and tuna live a few miles off shore.

From shore, try Clouser flies tied with brown, gray, blue, green or white. Fish around the rocks for cabrilla and pargo. Fish the down-current side of these rocks. In sandy bottom areas, use bigger patterns in light blue, gray or green (up to 5"). The common baitfish in this area are ballyhoo and sardina. Rip currents and undertow can be a problem, so don't fish from the beach if the waves and swells are large.

A great area to hide from the north wind, this bay is where you will first notice the Pacific Ocean's influence on the Sea of Cortez. More swell and wave action affects the beach fly fishing from about Los Frailes, down the peninsula, to Cabo San Lucas. Bahía Los Frailes is 21 miles (35 km) south of La Ribera, which is a short drive off Mexico 1, the main highway.

The main route to Los Frailes for most is from the Los Cabos Airport and north on Mexico 1. Take the turn off at Los Cuevas and follow the signs to La Ribera. Just before the town, look for the Punta Colorada sign. Take this paved road past Punta Colorada and then the dirt road past Cabo Pulmo, about 21 miles (35 km) from the La Ribera turnoff.

From San José del Cabo take Mexico 1 south, turn left on Calle Canseco to Boulevard Mijares. Then turn left on Calle Juarez and you're on the dirt road that passes La Playita and continues up the coast to Los Frailes.

Types of Fish
Shore: Over rocks - cabrilla, pargo, triggerfish, pompano and croaker. Sandy areas - jacks, rooster, pompano, ladyfish, giant needlefish, sierra, cornet fish.
Inshore: Dorado, wahoo, rooster, bonita, skipjack, sierra, jacks, pompano, triggerfish, needlefish along the drop-off.
Offshore: Marlin, sailfish, tuna, wahoo, dorado.

Equipment to Use - Shore
Rods: 8 to 10 weight, 9'.
Line: Sandy areas - full fly line (350 grain) or shooting head. Rock areas - intermediate or floating with sink-tip.
Leaders: 20 lb., non-tapered mono, 6'.
Reels: Direct or anti-reverse for saltwater use with disc drag system and quick take-apart feature for cleaning.
Other: Polarized sunglasses, stripping basket, foot protection, float tube or pontoon boat.

Equipment to Use - Inshore
Rods: 8 to 10 weight, 9'.
Line: Full fly line (450 grain), shooting head/intermediate.
Leaders: 20 lb., non-tapered mono, 6'. Short wire shock tippet for sierra.
Reels: Same as for shore or inshore.
Other: Polarized sunglasses, float tube or pontoon boat.

Equipment to Use - Offshore
Rods: 10 to 14 weight, 8' to 9'.
Line: Full fly line (650 grain), shooting head or intermediate. For billfish, 14 wt. rod, quality reel, lots of backing. If not interested in I.G.F.A. rules, use 125 lb., 36" bite tippet.
Leaders: 20 lb. with shock tippet for billfish.
Reels: Same as for inshore only larger.
Other: Polarized glasses, butt plate for fighting the big fish.

Flies to Use
Shore: Hook size 2/0 to 4/0, 1" to 4". Alf, Clouser, Bendback, Deceiver in white, gray, brown, blue or green, sardina, smelt. Use plenty of flash. Blue, green or white Popovics Surf Candy.
Inshore: Same as for shore.
Offshore: Large (6/0 hook) Alf, Clouser and streamers. For billfish, use Tandem Deceivers, Bill & Kate Howe Big Game Fly, El Tonto.

When to Fish
Shore: Low light a.m. and p.m. Incoming tides produce best action. Sight cast midday.
Inshore: Early morning, late afternoon.
Offshore: All day can be good. At slack tide, fish where you've seen the most fish that day.

Accommodations & Services
Hotel Bahía Frailes, (south side of bay) is full-service. To the north, Cabo Pulmo Beach Resort offers palapa-roofed, solar-powered cabanas by the day, week month. Camping on the beach is an option. Rent pangas from the Hotel Bahía Frailes. Other than the hotel restaurant, there are no other eating arrangements or stores in the area. At Cabo Pulmo, 8 km north, several restaurants but no markets.

Rating
This area is a 4 for shore and inshore fly fishing and a 7 for offshore fly angling.

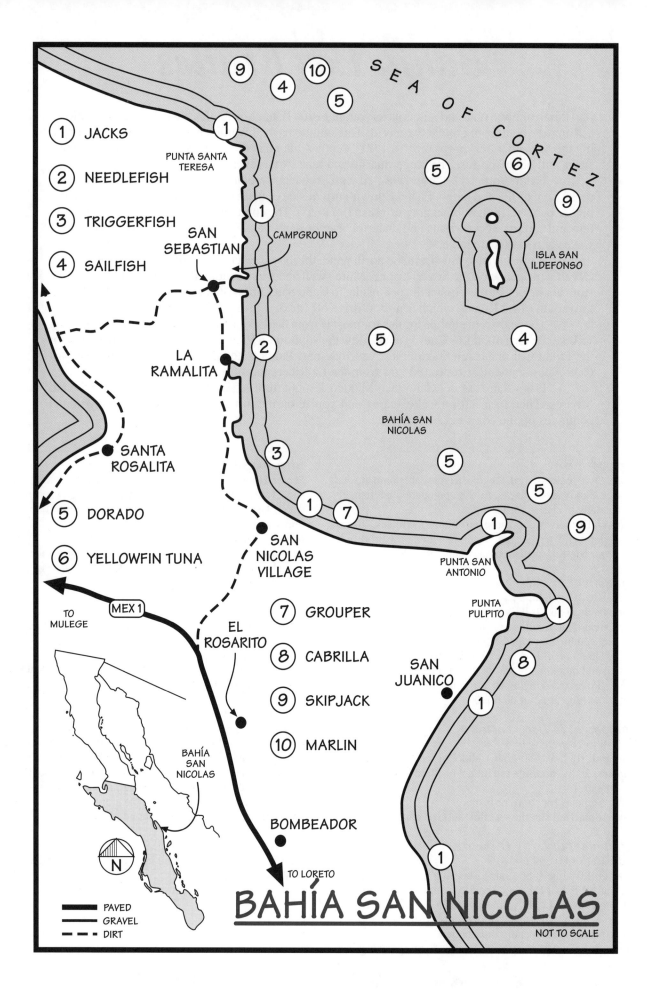

1 JACKS
2 NEEDLEFISH
3 TRIGGERFISH
4 SAILFISH
5 DORADO
6 YELLOWFIN TUNA
7 GROUPER
8 CABRILLA
9 SKIPJACK
10 MARLIN

PUNTA SANTA TERESA
SAN SEBASTIAN
CAMPGROUND
LA RAMALITA
SANTA ROSALITA
SAN NICOLAS VILLAGE
EL ROSARITO
BOMBEADOR

SEA OF CORTEZ
ISLA SAN ILDEFONSO
BAHÍA SAN NICOLAS
PUNTA SAN ANTONIO
PUNTA PULPITO
SAN JUANICO

MEX 1
TO MULEGE
TO LORETO

BAHÍA SAN NICOLAS

BAHÍA SAN NICOLAS

PAVED
GRAVEL
DIRT

NOT TO SCALE

N

Bahía San Nicolas

*T*his long, open bay is close to two large towns: Loreto to the south and Mulege to the north. Because it takes a bit of dirt road travel, this area is not very busy. Fishing along the shoreline of Bahía San Nicholas can be productive, but the real attraction here is off Isla San Ildefonso.

Dorado, sailfish, marlin, skipjack, yellowtail and yellowfin tuna are all around Ildefonso island. You can usually hire pangas in the small villages of San Nicolas and La Ramalita that can take you out to fish the shore-to-island waters. Driving to this area is a one-route option.

Driving north on Mexico 1 from Loreto, go to km 62. Turn right on a dirt road signed "San Nicolas 18." From here it is 13 miles (21 km) to the shore of the Sea Of Cortez. San Nicolas is a small fishing village that appears to be an oasis with many palm trees and greenery. Just before you enter the village you will see a dirt road that goes to the north. This road affords shoreline access for the next 4 miles. The other small fish camp along the way is La Ramalita. These villages are your only hope for hiring a panga to take you offshore.

The road ends at San Sebastian, 17 miles (27 km) from Mexico 1. Here you will find another primitive road that leads back to the highway. While the distance to the main road is about the same, as of this writing, I don't recommend using this road unless you have a 4-wheel-drive vehicle and plenty of time. I wouldn't go this way unless I had two vehicles in the group - one for backup.

Types of Fish
Shore: Rock areas, cabrilla, grouper, triggerfish, pompano and croaker. Sandy areas, jacks, rooster, pompano, ladyfish, giant needlefish, sierra.
Inshore: Dorado, rooster, bonito, sierra, jacks, barracuda, triggerfish, cornet fish, needlefish.
Offshore: Dorado, sailfish, marlin, skipjack, yellowtail and yellowfin tuna.

Equipment to Use - Shore
Rods: 7 to 10 weight, 9'.
Line: Sandy areas, full fly line (350 grain) or shooting head. Rock areas, intermediate or floating with sink-tip.
Leaders: 20 lb., non-tapered mono, 6'.
Reels: Direct or anti-reverse, designed for saltwater use with disc drag system and quick take-apart feature for cleaning.
Other: Polarized sunglasses, stripping basket, foot protection from rocks. Float tube or small inflatable pontoon boat.

Equipment to Use - Inshore
Rods: 8 to 11 weight, 9'.
Line: Full fly line (450 grain), shooting head/intermediate.
Leaders: 20 lb., non-tapered mono, 6'. Use short wire shock tippet for sierra and barracuda.
Reels: Same type as used from shore.
Other: Polarized sunglasses, float tube or small inflatable pontoon boat.

Equipment to Use - Offshore
Rods: 10 to 12 weight 8' - 9'. For billfish, 14 weight rod, quality reel with lots of backing. If not interested in I.G.F.A. rules use a 36" bite tippet of 125 lbs.
Line: Full fly line (650 grain), shooting head/intermediate.
Leaders: 20 lb. with shock tippet for billfish.
Reels: Same as above only larger and with more backing.
Other: Polarized sunglasses, butt plate for fighting big fish.

Flies to Use
Shore: Hook size 2/0 to 4/0, 1" to 4". White, gray, brown, blue and green Alf, Clouser, Bendback, Deceiver, sardina and smelt patterns. Use plenty of flash. Blue, green, or white Popovics Surf Candy.
Inshore: Same as for shore.
Offshore: Hook size 6/0, 4 - 8", Alf, Clouser and streamers. For billfish use Tandem Deceiver, Bill & Kate Howe Big Game Fly, El Tonto.

When to Fish
Shore: Low light a.m. and p.m. Incoming tides produce best action. Sight cast midday.
Inshore: Morning and late afternoon.
Offshore: All day can be good. At slack tide go where you've seen the most fish that day.

Accommodations & Services
Be self-contained, services are not available. Camp if you want to stay here. San Sebastian has a private campground. Return to Loreto, Conception Bay or Mulege for any services. The closest gas stations are in Loreto or Mulege.

Rating
This area is a 4 for shore and inshore fly fishing. Offshore it's a 7.

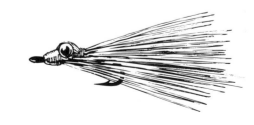

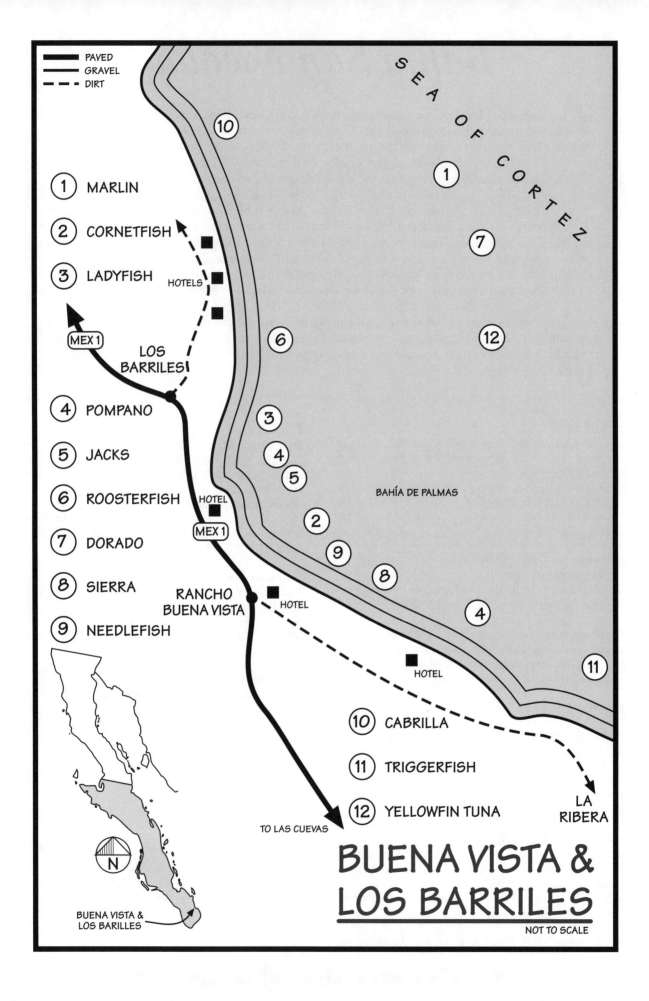

SEA OF CORTEZ

PAVED
GRAVEL
DIRT

① MARLIN
② CORNETFISH
③ LADYFISH
④ POMPANO
⑤ JACKS
⑥ ROOSTERFISH
⑦ DORADO
⑧ SIERRA
⑨ NEEDLEFISH
⑩ CABRILLA
⑪ TRIGGERFISH
⑫ YELLOWFIN TUNA

HOTELS

MEX 1

LOS BARRILES

HOTEL

MEX 1

RANCHO BUENA VISTA

HOTEL

HOTEL

BAHÍA DE PALMAS

LA RIBERA

TO LAS CUEVAS

BUENA VISTA & LOS BARRILES

NOT TO SCALE

N

BUENA VISTA & LOS BARILLES

Buena Vista & Los Barriles

*T*his area, considered the heart of the East Cape region, is only 45 minutes from the Los Cabos airport — most angler's point of arrival in southern Baja. The area offers a multitude of fly fishing options. With 10 miles of accessible beaches and a very deep marine drop-off a few miles off shore (the 100 fathom curve), the Buena Vista & Los Barriles area is one of Baja's most attractive fly fishing destinations.

Long sandy stretches of beach are interspersed with rocky points that are home to a variety of gamefish. Whether fishing the gray light before the sun comes up, sight casting midday, or fishing afternoons until the sun goes down, it's hard to find an area that offers so much fly fishing. Take a panga to the inshore waters where several rock reefs extend from beach. Looking down into the water here reminds one of an aquarium. There are a number of anchoring buoys placed on the bottom by hotels and locals. These buoys attract baitfish which in turn attract the larger fish. On many days these areas can be fished from a float tube or small inflatable pontoon boat.

Beyond the 100 fathom curve there are commercial shark buoys that often attract baitfish, that in turn attract dorado, tuna and skipjack. Also beyond the curve, the billfish, dorado and tuna hang out feeding on squid, mackerel, flying fish and sardina.

Types of Fish

Shore: Roosterfish swim within 20' of shore along with jacks, ladyfish, pargo, giant needlefish, cabrilla, triggerfish, pompano, sierra, shaped cornetfish.
Inshore: Dorado, rooster, bonita, skipjack, sierra, jacks, pompano, triggerfish and giant needlefish.
Offshore: Marlin, sailfish, tuna, wahoo and dorado.

Equipment to Use - Shore

Rods: 7 to 10 weight, 9'.
Lines: Sandy areas - full fly line (350 grain) or shooting head. Intermediate or floating with sink-tip for around the rocks.
Leaders: 20 lb. non-tapered mono, 6'.
Reels: Direct or anti-reverse, disc drag, designed for saltwater with quick take-apart feature for cleaning.
Other: Polarized sunglasses, stripping basket, foot protection from rocks. Float tube or small inflatable pontoon boat if conditions warrant.

Equipment to Use - Inshore

Rods: 8 - 11 weight, 9'.
Line: Full fly line (450 grain) shooting head/intermediate.
Leaders: Same as from shore. Short wire shock tippet for sierra.
Reels: Same as from shore.
Other: Float tube or small inflatable pontoon boat if desired.

Equipment to Use - Offshore

Rods: 10 - 14 weight, 8' - 9'.
Line: Full fly line (650 grain) shooting head system or intermediate.
Leaders: 20 lb. with shock tippet for billfish.
Reels: Same as for inshore only larger.
Other: Butt plate for fighting the big ones.

Flies to Use

Shore & inshore: Hook size 1/0 - 4/0, 1" - 4", Alf, Clouser, Deceiver in white, gray, brown, blue or green, sardina, smelt. Use plenty of flash. Blue, green, or white Popovics Surf Candy.
Offshore: Same as above plus heavy Clousers, size 6/0 hook. For billfish use Tandem Deceivers, Bill & Kate Howe Big Game Fly, El Tonto.

When to Fish

Shore: Early morning and late afternoon.
Offshore: All day is good. At slack tide, fish where you have seen the most fish that day.

Accommodations & Services

Rooms range from Club Med-like hotels with American-plan fine dining to beach camping. Large fleet of charter boats, cruisers and pangas available. Plenty of restaurants, markets, hardware stores, etc., in the town of Los Barriles. Diving, horse back riding, kayak rentals in the area.

Rating

The combination of good fishing, facilities, and easy accessibility, makes this a great place to start your Baja fly fishing adventures. Certain times of the year an 8 is a fair rating for the area.

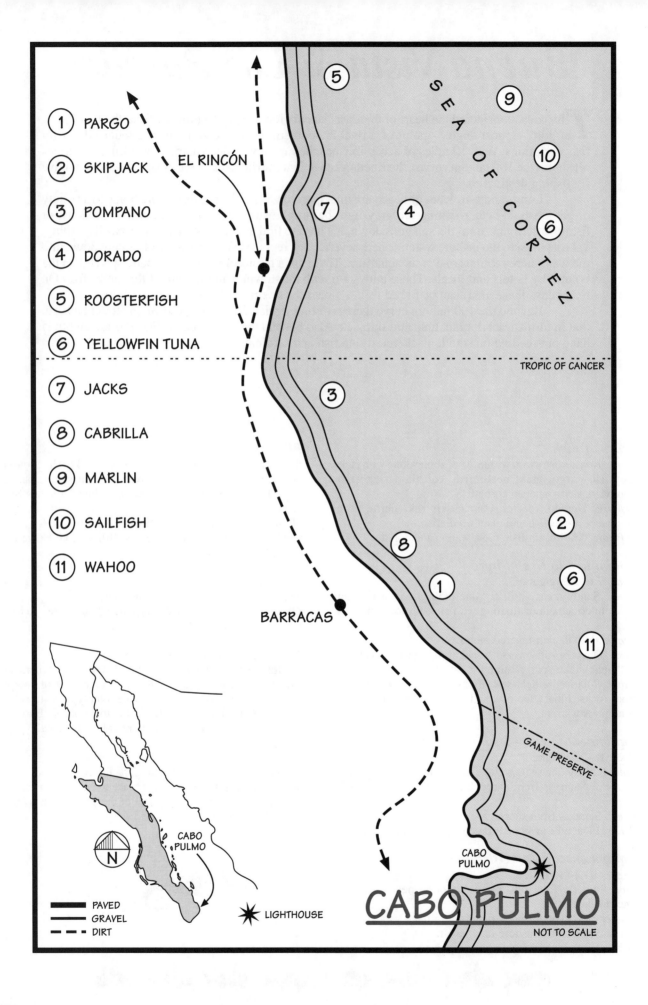

1. PARGO
2. SKIPJACK
3. POMPANO
4. DORADO
5. ROOSTERFISH
6. YELLOWFIN TUNA
7. JACKS
8. CABRILLA
9. MARLIN
10. SAILFISH
11. WAHOO

EL RINCÓN

SEA OF CORTEZ

TROPIC OF CANCER

GAME PRESERVE

BARRACAS

CABO PULMO

CABO PULMO

NOT TO SCALE

N

CABO PULMO

PAVED
GRAVEL
DIRT

LIGHTHOUSE

Cabo Pulmo

*A*mong other desirable features, Cabo Pulmo is at the outer limit of the cruising range of most fishing fleets. This means fewer boats, from either Cabo or East Cape, fish the area. Fly fishers usually appreciate solitude or, in southern Baja, less boat traffic.

Cabo Pulmo Reef is a designated game reserve. Fishing is not permitted on or around the reef. The beaches on both sides of the reef, however, are accessible and provide good fly fishing near the rock structure and sandy areas.

Around the rocks, try small Clouser flies in brown, gray and blue. Also look for cabrilla, lookdowns and pargo feeding among these rocks. Remember to fish the down-current side of the rocks first. On the sandy areas try bigger fly patterns (up to 5") in light blue, gray or green. A common baitfish in this area is ballyhoo that are a little longer than sardina. Hiring a boat can provide the fly angler great inshore and offshore opportunities. There are a few pangas available for rent in the area.

Access Cabo Pulmo from the road and same turn-off one takes to Punta Colorada. Drive approximately 17 miles (26 km) south of La Ribera, on a mostly paved road. It becomes dirt for the last few miles just before the village of Cabo Pulmo. From Cabo Pulmo one has access to the entire Bahía Pulmo area.

Types of Fish
Shore: Rock areas, cabrilla, pargo, triggerfish, pompano, croaker, etc. Sandy bottom areas, jacks, rooster, pompano, ladyfish, giant needlefish, sierra, cornetfish.
Inshore: Dorado, wahoo, rooster, bonita, skipjack, sierra, jacks, pompano, triggerfish and giant needlefish along the drop-off.
Offshore: Marlin, sailfish, tuna, wahoo and dorado.

Equipment to Use - Shore
Rods: 7 to 10 weight, 9'.
Line: Full fly line (350 grain) or shooting head system. Sandy areas, intermediate or floating. Sink-tip for around the rocks.
Leaders: 20 lb., non-taper mono, 6'. Smaller if you aren't getting strikes.
Reels: Direct or anti-reverse, disc drag, for saltwater. Quick take-apart feature for easy cleaning.
Other: Stripping basket, polarized sunglasses, foot protection. Float tube or small inflatable pontoon boat if desired.

Equipment to Use - Inshore
Rods: 8 to 11 weight, 9'.
Line: Full fly line (450 grain), shooting head system or intermediate.
Leaders: 20 lb., non-tapered mono, 6'. Short wire shock tippet for sierra and barracuda.
Reels: Same as used from shore.
Other: Float tube or small inflatable pontoon boat if desired.

Equipment to Use - Offshore
Rods: 10 to 14 weight, 8' - 9'.
Line: Full fly line (650 grain) shooting head/intermediate.
Leaders: 20 lb., use a shock tippet for billfish.
Reels: Same as used for inshore only larger.
Other: For billfish bring a 14 wt. rod, quality reel with lots of backing. If you're not interested in I.G.F.A. rules or setting a record, try a 125 lb., 36" bite tippet. Use a butt plate for fighting the big guys.

Flies to Use
Shore: Hook size 2/0 - 4/0, 1" - 4", Alf, Clouser, Bendback, Deceiver in white, gray, brown, blues or green, sardina, smelt. Use plenty of flash. Blue, green, or white Popovics Surf Candy.
Inshore: Same as for the beach area.
Offshore: Large Alf, Clousers and streamers. For billfish, Tandem Deceivers, Bill & Kate Howe Big Game Fly, El Tonto.

When to Fish
Shore: Low light a.m. and p.m. Incoming tides produce best action. Sight cast midday.
Inshore: I prefer early mornings and late afternoons. All day can be good. At slack tide try to fish where you've seen the most fish that day.

Accommodations & Services
Cabo Pulmo Beach Resort offers palapa-roofed, solar powered cabanas by the day, week or month. Camping on the beach is an option. Dive services are available here. There are a few restaurants and one bar in the area, but the nearest markets, services and gas stations are in the town of La Ribera.

Rating:
This area is a 5 for the shore, an 8 for inshore and offshore fly fishing.

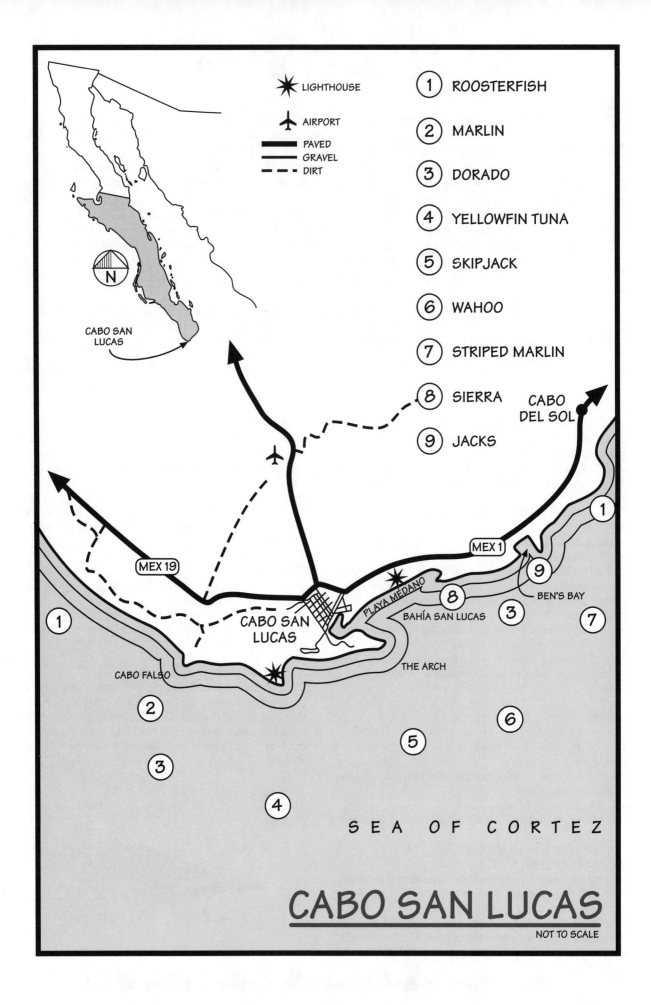

LIGHTHOUSE

AIRPORT

PAVED
GRAVEL
DIRT

1 ROOSTERFISH

2 MARLIN

3 DORADO

4 YELLOWFIN TUNA

5 SKIPJACK

6 WAHOO

7 STRIPED MARLIN

8 SIERRA

9 JACKS

N

CABO SAN LUCAS

CABO DEL SOL

MEX 1

MEX 19

CABO SAN LUCAS

PLAYA MEDANO

BAHÍA SAN LUCAS

BEN'S BAY

THE ARCH

CABO FALSO

SEA OF CORTEZ

CABO SAN LUCAS

NOT TO SCALE

Cabo San Lucas
The Corridor

*C*abo San Lucas, long considered the marlin capital of the world, has over 50,000 marlin, sailfish, and swordfish hooked a year. This is the place to go to catch a billfish with a fly rod.

There are several companies in the region that cater to the fly fisher (see appendix). All have trained crews to assist in your pursuit of billfish on a flyrod. Tuna, dorado, wahoo and roosterfish provide exceptional fly rod action as well.

Beach fishing along the corridor can be exciting too. With over 16 vehicle-accessible beaches between San José Del Cabo and Cabo San Lucas, the adventurous fly fisher can spend an entire vacation exploring and fly fishing the shoreline and these beautiful beaches. Each is near or separates a hotel of resort of some kind, so amenities are nearby.

Around rocks, fish for porgy, pompano using small brown, gray, or blue Clouser flies. Fish the down current side of rocks. Sand bottom waters, use 5" patterns in light blue, gray or green. Ballyhoo and sardina are common baitfish along The Corridor.

A word of caution: these beaches have steep breaks with sharp drop-offs and often the undertow can be a problem. Don't try beach fishing if the waves and swell are large. I don't recommend float tubes or inflatable pontoon boats in this area. The influence of the Pacific Ocean can cause large swells, waves and undertows. This makes using these craft dangerous.

Types of Fish
Shore: Rock areas - cabrilla, pargo, triggerfish, pompano, croaker and others. Sandy areas - jacks, rooster, pompano, ladyfish, giant needlefish, sierra.
Inshore: Dorado, wahoo, rooster, bonita, skipjack, sierra, jacks, pompano, triggerfish, giant needlefish along the drop-off.
Offshore: Marlin, sailfish, tuna, wahoo and dorado.

Equipment to Use - Shore
Rods: 8 to 10 weight, 9'.
Line: Full fly line (350 grain) or shooting head. Sandy areas, intermediate or floating. Sink-tip for around rocks.
Leaders: 20 lb., non-taper mono, 6'.
Reels: Saltwater direct or anti-reverse, disc drag with quick take-apart for cleaning.
Other: Polarized sunglasses, stripping basket, foot protection from rocks.

Equipment to Use - Inshore
Rods: 8 to 11 weight, 9'.
Line: Full fly line (450 grain) shooting head/intermediate.
Leaders: Same as for shore. Short wire shock tippet for sierra, barracuda.
Reels: Same as for shore.

Equipment to Use - Offshore
Rods: 10 - 14 weight, 8' - 9'.
Line: Full fly line (650 grain) shooting head system or intermediate. For billfish, 14 wt. rod, quality reel with lots of backing.
Leaders: 20 lb. with 125 lb. shock tippet for billfish.
Reels: Same as above only larger.
Other: Polarized sunglasses, butt plate for fighting big fish.

Flies to Use - Beach
Shore: 2/0 - 4/0 hook, 1" - 4" white, gray, brown, blue or green Alf, Clouser, Bendback, Deceiver, sardina and smelt. Tie plenty of flash. Popovics Surf Candy, blue, green or white.
Inshore: Same as for the shore (above).
Offshore: Large Alf, Clouser and streamers. For billfish, Tandem Deceiver, Bill & Kate Howe Big Game Fly, El Tonto, large streamers.

When to Fish
Shore: Low light, a.m. and p.m. Better action on incoming tide. Midday best for sight casting.
Inshore: Early morning and late afternoon.
Offshore: All day. At slack tide, fish where you've seen the most fish that day.

Accommodations & Services
Hotels, condos, trailer parks for every budget all along this coastline. All services, stores, charter boats in Cabo San Lucas and San José Del Cabo. Baja Anglers, Minervas, and Cortez Yacht Charters cater to the fly fisher.

Rating
With the difficulty caused by the high surf, undertow and drop-offs this area is a 3 for beach fly fishing. Off and inshore rates a 7 because of the volume of billfish and fleet availability.

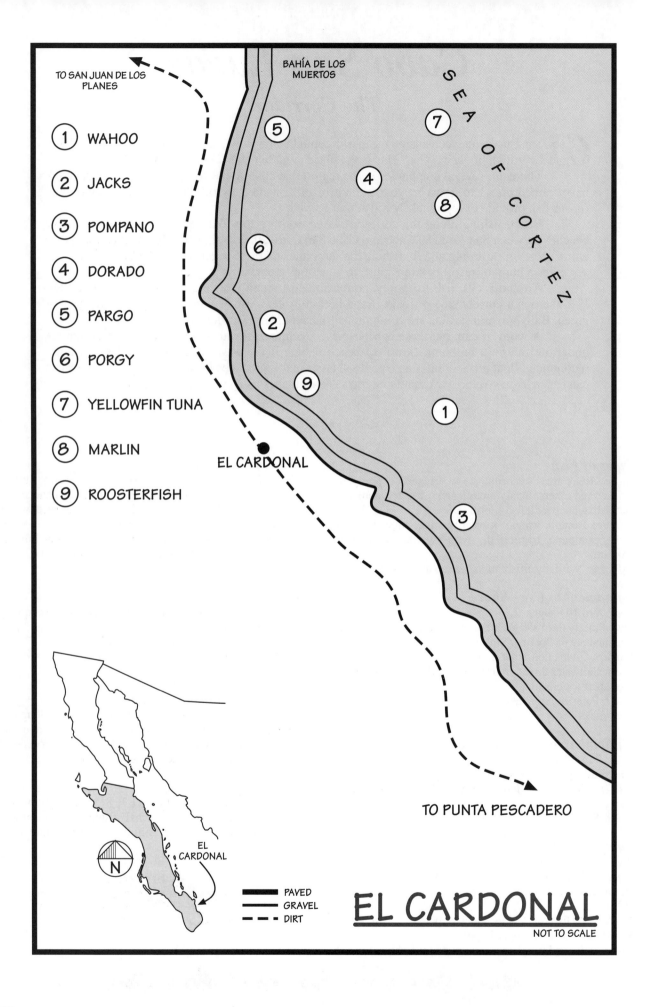

TO SAN JUAN DE LOS
PLANES

BAHÍA DE LOS MUERTOS

SEA OF CORTEZ

1 WAHOO
2 JACKS
3 POMPANO
4 DORADO
5 PARGO
6 PORGY
7 YELLOWFIN TUNA
8 MARLIN
9 ROOSTERFISH

EL CARDONAL

TO PUNTA PESCADERO

EL CARDONAL

N

PAVED
GRAVEL
DIRT

EL CARDONAL

NOT TO SCALE

El Cardonal

With unspoiled vistas and spectacular rock cliffs, this spot is a "must" for anglers interested in exploring and fishing a remote area in Baja. You'll find a few sandy beaches here but the area is primarily rocky coastline. Carry everything needed for the day, especially water, and wear good shoes for some rock hopping.

There are a number of areas to fly fish that you'll probably have to yourself. With the exception of a few local anglers, these areas haven't seen much tackle, let alone a fly. It all adds up to unique fly fishing, inaccessibility and solitude.

Along the sandy beaches a number of gamefish are available and occasionally seen feeding in the rocky areas. The cabrilla, grouper, pargo, triggerfish and other species (that require a fish field book to identify) will occupy your time between fish feedings.

To reach El Cardonal get on Mexico 1. If coming from La Paz, drive south about 68 miles (110 km). From the Los Cabos airport go north about 46 miles (75 km) and turn, at the sign, into Los Barriles. Turn left at the "T" after the speed bump at the north end of town. This dirt road winds along the shore 8 miles (14 km) to Punta Pescadero. After another 4 miles (6 km) you reach El Cardonal. This road follows the coast for another 8 miles (13 km) providing access to more secluded fly fishing spots. Continue on this dirt road and you end up on pavement at Los Planes. Don't drive the rough road (farther than Los Primeros Piedras) without 4-wheel drive.

Types of Fish
Shore: Rooster, jacks, ladyfish, giant needlefish, pompano, sierra.
Inshore: Dorado, rooster, bonita, skipjack, sierra, jacks, pompano, triggerfish and giant needlefish.
Offshore: Marlin, sailfish, tuna, wahoo, dorado.

Equipment to Use - Shore
Rods: 7 to 10 weight 9'.
Line: Rocks - intermediate or floating with sink-tip. Intermediate for the few sandy beaches.
Leaders: 20 lb., non-tapered mono, 6'.
Reels: Saltwater direct or anti-reverse, disc drag with quick take-apart for cleaning.
Other: Polarized sunglasses, stripping basket, foot protection from the rocks, float tube or pontoon boat if desired.

Equipment to Use - Inshore
Rods: 8 to 11 weight 9'.
Line: Full fly line (450 grain) shooting head/intermediate.
Leaders: Same as for shore. Short wire shock tippet for sierra.
Reels: Same as for shore.
Other: Polarized sunglasses, float tube or small inflatable pontoon boat.

Equipment to Use - Offshore
Rods: 10 - 14 weight, 8' - 9'.
Line: Full fly line (650 grain) shooting head/intermediate.
Leaders: 20 lb. with shock tippet for billfish.
Reels: Same system as for inshore only larger.
Other: Polarized sunglasses, butt plate for fighting big fish.

Flies to Use
Shore: 2/0 - 4/0 hook, 1" - 4" white, gray, brown, blues or green Clouser, Deceiver, Alf, sardina, smelt. Use plenty of flash. Popovics Surf Candy in blue, green, white, sand eels in baitfish colors.
Inshore: 1/0 to 4/0 hook, 1" - 4" same flies as used for tuna and from shore.
Offshore: Same as above, plus heavy Clousers (7/0 hook) For billfish: Tandem Deceiver, Bill & Kate Howe Big Game Fly, El Tonto.

When to Fish
Shore: Winter, with protection from the north wind, can be great. Early Spring - Fall is good, skip September because of chubascos (hurricanes). I prefer early morning first, then late afternoon.
Offshore: A year-round fishery. April - August and October - November 15th is the best time. Fish all day. At slack tide, return to where you saw the most fish that day.

Accommodations & Services
Los Barriles is the closest town and has everything you need including several markets, restaurants and a hardware store. Gasoline station on Mexico 1, down the road at Buena Vista. Some services at Hotel Punta Pescadero. El Cardonal has several small stores and a small hotel offering meals.

Rating
This area rates a 4 year round. During peak fly fishing times a 7 is a fair rating.

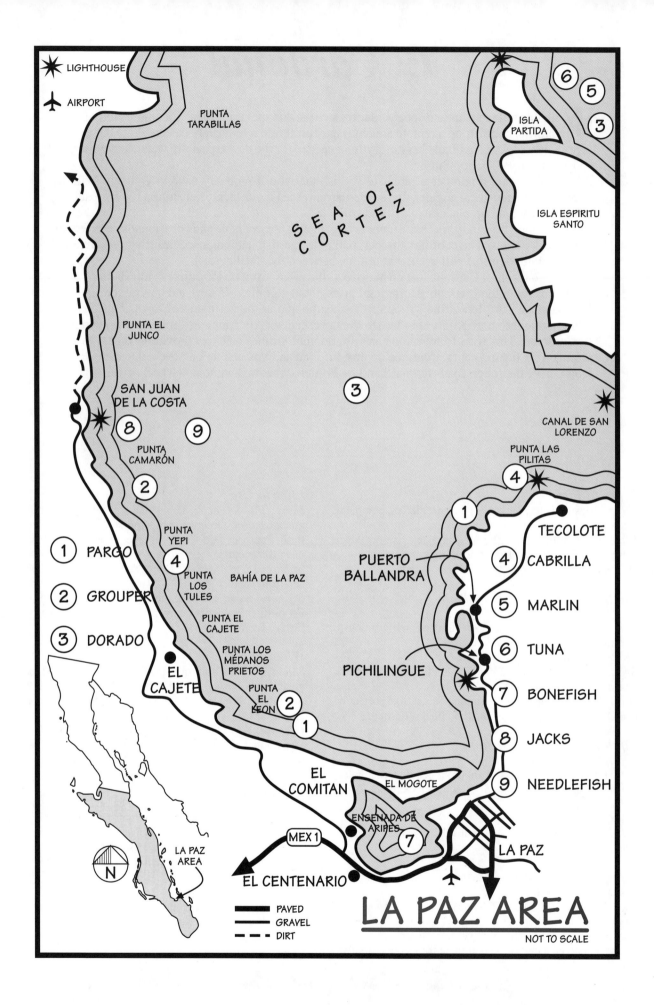

LIGHTHOUSE
AIRPORT

PUNTA
TARABILLAS

SEA OF
CORTEZ

ISLA
PARTIDA

ISLA ESPIRITU
SANTO

6
5
3

PUNTA EL
JUNCO

SAN JUAN
DE LA COSTA

CANAL DE SAN
LORENZO

8
9

PUNTA
CAMARÓN

2

PUNTA LAS
PILITAS

4

1

PUNTA
YEPI

BAHÍA DE LA PAZ

PUERTO
BALLANDRA

TECOLOTE

1 PARGO

4

PUNTA
LOS
TULES

4 CABRILLA

2 GROUPER

PUNTA EL
CAJETE

5 MARLIN

PICHILINGUE

3 DORADO

PUNTA LOS
MÉDANOS
PRIETOS

6 TUNA

EL
CAJETE

PUNTA
EL
LEON

7 BONEFISH

2

8 JACKS

1

9 NEEDLEFISH

EL
COMITAN

EL MOGOTE

ENSENADA DE
ARIPES

7

LA PAZ

MEX 1

LA PAZ
AREA

EL CENTENARIO

N

PAVED
GRAVEL
DIRT

LA PAZ AREA

NOT TO SCALE

La Paz Area

*T*he area around La Paz, capital of Baja California Sur, offers a variety of fly fishing venues and is a good base for jaunts to several other locations featured in this guidebook. This city of 160,000 has managed to retain much of its Mexican charm. It is 125 miles (200 km) north of Cabo San Lucas, which is becoming more tourist oriented by the minute. There is plenty to do in La Paz, too.

Non-fishing family members can enjoy the sights, scenes, and shopping in this vibrant city while the fly fisher can rent a car or hire a cab and travel a scant 20 miles out to Punta Las Pilitas. You'll find deserted beaches with rocky shorelines and an assortment of fish species including cabrilla, pargo, rooster, bonito, sierra, jacks and corvina.

Working your way back toward town, you will find other beaches and coves with exotic names like Tecolote and Balandra. These offer sandy and rocky beaches and even some with thick mangroves. Reports of bonefish taken in El Mogote are intriguing. The areas closer to town are fished extensively and will not provide the wide-open action for which one has traveled.

That said, you still never know what you might find right in La Paz. The channel in front of the Malecon (the walkway next to the sea in front of the hotels and businesses) can provide action if you fish where there are diving birds feeding on baitfish.

Cabrilla and pargo often feed around the rocks. Fish with small brown, gray or blue Clouser flies. Try larger patterns in light blue, gray or green (up to 5") over sandy areas. This will mimic sardina and ballyhoo, common area baitfish.

There are pangas available in town as well as at Playa Tecolote. Cruisers are also available for offshore fishing beyond Isla Espiritu Santo and Isla Partida. Charter boat contact numbers are in the back of this guide or simply ask around when you get to La Paz.

Types of Fish
Shore: Rock areas - cabrilla, pargo, triggerfish, pompano, croaker. Sandy areas - jacks, rooster, pompano, ladyfish, giant needlefish, sierra, corvina.
Inshore (within Bahía De La Paz): Rooster, bonito, sierra, jacks, corvina, triggerfish, snook.
Offshore: Marlin, sailfish, tuna, wahoo, dorado.

Equipment to Use - Shore
Rods: 7 to 10 weight, 9'.
Line: Sandy areas, full fly line (350 grain) or shooting head. Intermediate or floating with sink-tip for around the rocks.
Leaders: 20 lb., non-tapered mono, 6'.
Reels: Direct or anti-reverse model designed for saltwater, with disc drag system and quick take-apart feature for easy cleaning.
Other: Polarized sunglasses, stripping basket, foot protection from rocks. Float tube or small inflatable pontoon boat, but, because of boating activity, this can be difficult.

Equipment to Use - Inshore
Rods: 8 to 11 weight, 9'.
Line: Full fly line (450 grain), shooting head system or intermediate.
Leaders: 20 lb., non-tapered mono, 6'. Use short wire shock tippet for sierra.
Reels: Same as used from shore.
Other: Polarized sunglasses, float tube or small inflatable pontoon boat.

Equipment to Use - Offshore
Rods: 10 to 14 weight, 8' to 9'.
Line: Full fly line (650 grain) shooting head system or intermediate. For billfish 14 weight rod, quality reel, lots of backing. For non I.G.F.A. rules use 125 lb., 36" bite tippet.
Leaders: 20 lb. with shock tippet for billfish.
Reels: Same as for shore only larger.
Other: Polarized sunglasses, butt plate for the big fish.

Flies to Use
Shore: 2/0 to 4/0 hook, 1" to 4", Alf, Clouser, Bendback, Deceiver in white, gray, brown, blue or green, sardina and smelt with plenty of flash. Blue, green, or white Popovics Surf Candy.
Inshore, within Bahía De La Paz: Same as for shore.
Offshore: Large Alf, Clouser and streamers. For billfish, Tandem Deceivers, Bill & Kate Howe Big Game Fly, El Tonto.

When to Fish
Shore: Low light morning and afternoon, especially on incoming tides. Sight cast midday.
Inshore, within Bahía De La Paz: Early a.m. and late p.m.
Offshore: All day can be good. At slack tide try where you have seen fish that day.

Accommodations & Services
There are lots of bay-view choices along the Malecon and other fine hotels away from the water. A full range of shops and services are available here.

Rating
This area is a strong 5 for the beach and bay. Offshore is a 6.

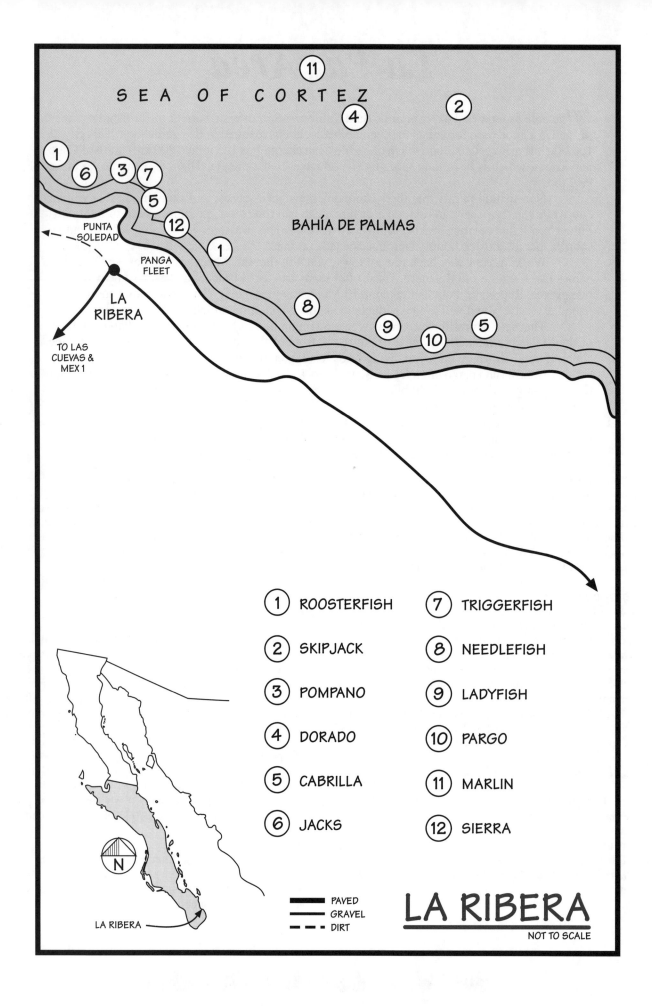

SEA OF CORTEZ

BAHÍA DE PALMAS

PUNTA SOLEDAD

PANGA FLEET

LA RIBERA

TO LAS CUEVAS & MEX 1

1 ROOSTERFISH
2 SKIPJACK
3 POMPANO
4 DORADO
5 CABRILLA
6 JACKS

7 TRIGGERFISH
8 NEEDLEFISH
9 LADYFISH
10 PARGO
11 MARLIN
12 SIERRA

N

LA RIBERA

PAVED
GRAVEL
DIRT

LA RIBERA

NOT TO SCALE

La Ribera

*H*ere's another Baja fly fishing getaway that's fairly secluded yet has rather easy access. Go six miles off Mexico 1, the main highway from Los Cabos airport (going north) and take the turnoff at Las Cuevas. Follow the signs to La Ribera. Here there are sandy beaches, several rock reefs and a few rocky points (to the southeast) that will challenge fly fishers who like to walk and cast.

The road is paved to the town of La Ribera and the beach is accessed from a well-traveled dirt road east of the town. At the end of the access road is a small fleet of pangas, the 24' open skiffs that are exceptionally fly rod friendly. You may be able to hire one for fishing in or offshore.

Directly in front of town, offshore, commercial shark buoys provide baitfish cover. A variety of the predatory gamefish will take the fly. Spring to early summer sardina are often found close to the shore. The indicator is when locals fish with bait from the beach. Summertime this offshore area, with its deep-water canyons, is the undisputed home of the challenging blue marlin. Many of these magnificent billfish reach 1,000 lbs. or more.

North of La Ribera, a point and rock reef extends 1/4 mile into the bay. Start here early in the morning using a crab pattern. Work it slowly back and forth on the reef, while looking for baitfish, birds or boiling fish. If nothing's biting, work the beach toward town using a brown or white Clouser tied with flash.

If there is any kind of swell, try to cast at the same angle as the swell moves down the beach. Be careful how long you let the fly sink. You can lose more flies on the rock strewn bottom than you can carry. If you want more, travel south down a dirt road signed "Punta Colorada". You'll find beach and fishing access at several turnoffs.

Types of Fish
Shore: Rock areas - cabrilla, pargo, triggerfish, croaker. Sandy areas - jacks, ladyfish, pompano, giant needlefish, sierra, cornetfish.
Inshore: Dorado, rooster, bonita, skipjack, sierra, jacks, pompano, triggerfish, giant needlefish along the color line.
Offshore: Marlin, sailfish, tuna, wahoo and dorado.

Equipment to Use - Shore
Rods: 7 to 10 weight, 9'.
Line: Sandy areas - full line (350 grain) or shooting head. Rock areas - intermediate, floating or sink-tip.
Leaders: Non-tapered mono 6'. Start with 20 lb.
Reels: Direct or anti-reverse disc drag for saltwater. A quick take-apart eases cleaning.
Other: Stripping basket, foot protection for the rocks. Float tube or small inflatable pontoon boat.

Equipment to Use - Inshore
Rods: 8 to 11 weight, 9'.
Line: Full fly line (450 grain) shooting head or intermediate.
Leaders: 20 lb. non-tapered mono, 6'. Short wire shock tippet for sierra.
Reels: Same as for shore.
Other: Float tube or small inflatable pontoon.

Equipment to Use - Offshore
Rods: 10 to 14 weight, 8' - 9'.
Line: Full fly line (650 grain) shooting head/intermediate. For blue marlin, 14 weight, quality reel, lots of backing and 125 lb., 36" bite tippet.
Leaders: 20 lb., with shock tippet for billfish.

Reels: Same as for shore only bigger.
Other: Butt plate for fighting bigger fish.

Flies to Use
Shore & Inshore: 1/0 - 4/0 hook, 1" - 4", white, gray, brown, blue or green Alf, Clouser, Deceiver, sardina and smelt patterns. Tie with plenty of flash. Blue, green or white Popovics Surf Candy. On the reef try a crab pattern.
Offshore: Same as above plus heavy Clousers (#7 hook) to get down deep around the buoys. For billfish, Tandem Deceivers, Bill & Kate Howe Big Game Fly, El Tonto.

When to Fish
Shore: Many times, early mornings you can hear the fish feeding! Low light morning and afternoon and incoming tides. Sight cast midday.
Inshore: I prefer early morning and late afternoon.
Offshore: All day can be good. At slack tide try to fish where you've seen the most fish that day.

Accommodations & Services
Best at Buena Vista and Los Barriles. Markets, restaurants, taco stands, La Capilla trailer park north on the dirt road signed Rancho Leonero. Pemex gas station to the southeast at the edge of town.

Rating
This area is a strong 6 for shore, inshore and offshore.

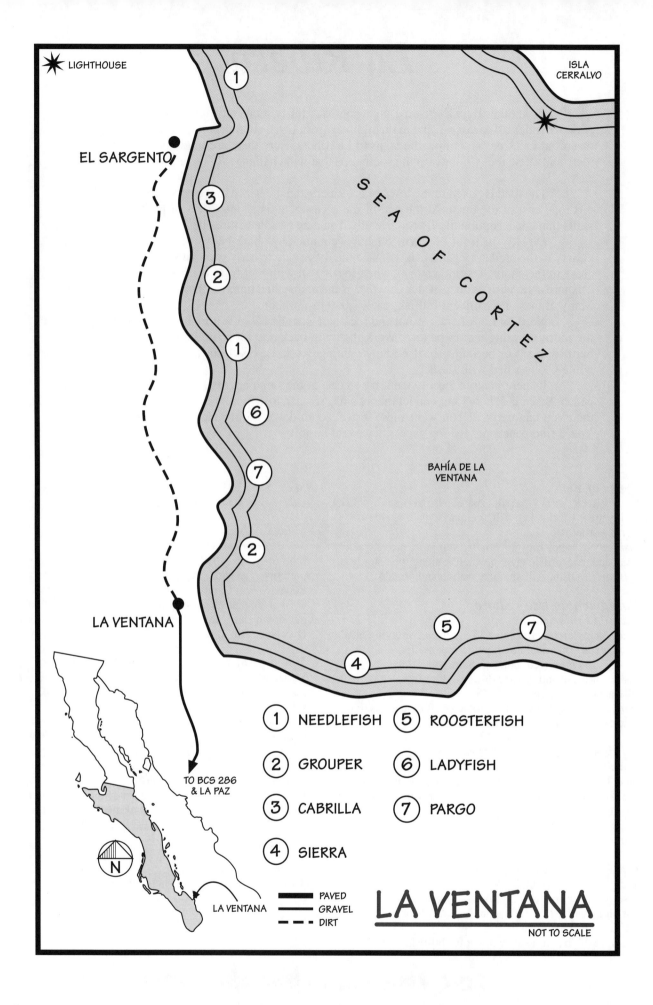

LIGHTHOUSE

ISLA CERRALVO

EL SARGENTO

SEA OF CORTEZ

BAHÍA DE LA VENTANA

LA VENTANA

TO BCS 286 & LA PAZ

LA VENTANA

①	NEEDLEFISH	⑤	ROOSTERFISH
②	GROUPER	⑥	LADYFISH
③	CABRILLA	⑦	PARGO
④	SIERRA		

PAVED
GRAVEL
DIRT

LA VENTANA
NOT TO SCALE

La Ventana to El Sargento

*H*ere's an easy day trip from La Paz with over 20 miles of white sandy beach. Sight casting is the game here as this is a perfect area to stroll while searching for fish. Look for dark shadows moving in the water parallel to the shoreline. Then cast your fly out in front of that moving shadow. If you've guessed right and the shadow is hungry or curious, hold on!

The rocky areas, particularly to the north towards El Sargento seem to hold fish all year long. The resident rockfish will provide plenty of action when the fishing is slow from the beaches. Another option if the action is slow, is casting to the few areas where the sand bottom turns to rock. If you don't want to walk, try inshore or bluewater fishing. Both villages have small panga fleets that will take you out for a few hours or for the day.

To get to these areas, follow the same directions used to get from La Paz to Las Arenas, i.e. Highway 286 south. At km 38, make a left turn which sends you north. Approximately 5 miles (8 km) farther down this road you arrive at the village of La Ventana, situated on the shore of Bahía de la Ventana. An "L" shaped bay, opening to the Sea of Cortez lies to the east. Canal de Cerralvo is on the north. Seven miles offshore is Isla Cerralvo, a 17 mile long island that offers some protection for the entire bay.

Types of Fish
Shore: Sandy beaches - rooster, jacks, ladyfish, giant needlefish, pompano, sierra. Look for rockfish near the rocks.
Inshore: Dorado, rooster, bonito, skipjack, sierra, jacks, pompano, triggerfish and giant needlefish are common throughout this area in the bay.
Offshore: A few miles out it's over 1,000' deep so conceivably all major bluewater species are available.

Equipment to Use - Shore
Rods: 7 to 10 weight, 9'.
Line: Intermediate or floating with sink-tip for around rocks. Intermediate also in the few sandy areas.
Leaders: 20 lb., non-tapered mono, 6'.
Reels: Direct or anti-reverse, disc drag, for saltwater, quick take-apart for cleaning.
Other: Polarized sunglasses, stripping basket and foot protection from rocks. Float tube or pontoon boat.

Equipment to Use - Inshore
Rods: 8 to 11 weight, 9'.
Line: Full fly line (450 grain) shooting head or intermediate.
Leaders: 20 lb. non-tapered mono, 6'. Short wire shock tippet for sierra.
Reels: Same as for shore.
Other: Same as for shore

Equipment to Use - Offshore
Rods: 10 to 14 weight, 8' - 9'.
Line: Full fly line (650 grain) shooting head or intermediate.
Leaders: 20 lb. with shock tippet for billfish.
Reels: Same as for inshore only larger.
Other: Polarized sunglasses, fighting butt for the big fish.

Flies to Use
Shore: 2/0 to 4/0, 1" - 4" Clouser, Deceiver, Alf, in white, gray, brown, blue or green, sardina, smelt. Tie plenty of flash. Blue, green or white Popovics Surf Candy, sand eels in baitfish colors.
Inshore: Same as shore patterns.
Offshore: Same as above, plus heavy Clousers (#7 hook). For billfish - Tandem Deceiver, Bill & Kate Howe Big Game Fly, El Tonto.

When to Fish
Shore: Hot summer has hot fishing. Spring and fall favored with cooler weather. Winter fishing just good.
Inshore & offshore: Good year around. April to August and October to Mid-November are best.

Accommodations & Services
La Paz, 30 minutes away, has all services. Rooms range from campgrounds to 5 star hotels. Beach camping just north of La Ventana, next to the old pier.

Rating
Summer and fall an 8 for all areas. Winter is a 6 for all areas.

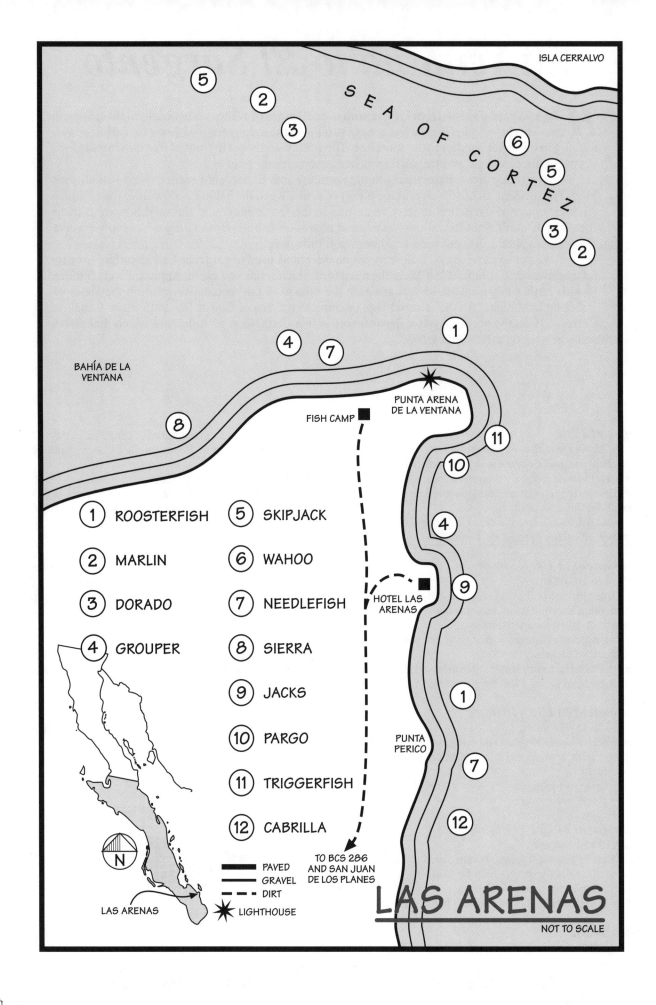

ISLA CERRALVO

SEA OF CORTEZ

BAHÍA DE LA
VENTANA

FISH CAMP

PUNTA ARENA
DE LA VENTANA

HOTEL LAS
ARENAS

PUNTA
PERICO

TO BCS 286
AND SAN JUAN
DE LOS PLANES

(1) ROOSTERFISH

(2) MARLIN

(3) DORADO

(4) GROUPER

(5) SKIPJACK

(6) WAHOO

(7) NEEDLEFISH

(8) SIERRA

(9) JACKS

(10) PARGO

(11) TRIGGERFISH

(12) CABRILLA

LAS ARENAS

N

PAVED
GRAVEL
DIRT
LIGHTHOUSE

LAS ARENAS

NOT TO SCALE

Las Arenas

*T*his area has it all: expansive east and west beaches, outstanding inshore and offshore fishing and what many consider to be the best rooster fishing area in all Baja. All this fly fishing is accessible on foot or from a panga.

For offshore action, hire a panga or cruiser and you can be fishing in about 20 minutes. A 1,000' deep trench runs between Isla Cerralvo and the shore, through which all bluewater species travel on their migration to and from the Sea of Cortez.

Near the south tip of the island a shelf extends 3/4 of a mile in the Sea of Cortez. You never know what fish are under the diving birds here. Some are large resident seabass, tuna, skipjack, wahoo, and even dorado and marlin on the edges of the reef. These fish crash on sardina meatballs while birds dive into the melee. If marlin are feeding it's sometimes possible to sight cast to them without teasing the fish to the boat. Just ease the boat up to the feeding fish, throw a few sardinas out to keep them up top, and then cast a big streamer into the frenzy. This area will not disappoint you.

By car, from either Mexico 1 at San Antonio or Highway 286 from La Paz, drive as if heading for Los Muertos. Three miles (5 km) before Los Muertos turn left and go some 5 miles (8 km) to the beach and large panga fleet. Another road off to the right leads to the Las Arenas Resort. Around the point (Punta Perico) and beyond the hotel, the shoreline becomes rocky. Here you will find several shallow rock reefs that usually have grouper, cabrilla, triggerfish, pargo and ladyfish lurking about.

Types of Fish
Shore: Sandy beach east and west around point to lighthouse, rooster, jacks, ladyfish, giant needlefish, pompano, sierra. Point area - rockfish.
Inshore: Dorado, roosterfish, bonita, skipjack, sierra, jacks, pompano, triggerfish, giant needlefish.
Offshore: All major bluewater species possible.

Equipment to Use - Shore
Rods: 7 to 10 weight, 9'.
Line: Intermediate or floating with sink-tip around rocks. Intermediate also on sandy beaches.
Leaders: 20 lb., non-tapered mono, 6'.
Reels: Direct or anti-reverse, disc drag for saltwater, quick take-apart for cleaning.
Other: Polarized sunglasses, stripping basket, foot protection from rocks. Float tube or pontoon boat.

Equipment to Use - Inshore
Rods: 8 to 11 weight, 9'.
Line: Full fly line (450 grain) shooting head system or intermediate.
Leaders: 20 lb., non-tapered mono, 6'. Short wire shock tippet for sierra and barracuda.
Reels: Same as for shore.
Other: Same as for shore.

Equipment to Use - Offshore
Rods: 10 to 14 weight, 8' - 9'.
Line: Full fly line (650 grain) shooting head/intermediate.
Leaders: 20 lb. with shock tippet for billfish.
Reels: Large direct or anti-reverse with disc drag for saltwater.
Other: Polarized sunglasses, butt plate for fighting big ones.

Flies to Use
Shore: 2/0 to 4/0 hook, 1" - 4" Clouser, Deceiver, Alf, in white, gray, brown, blues or green, sardina, smelt. Use plenty of flash. Blue, green or white Popovics Surf Candy, sand eel in baitfish colors.
Inshore: Same as from shore.
Offshore: Same as above, plus heavy Clousers (#7 hook). For billfish - Tandem Deceiver, Bill & Kate Howe Big Game Fly, El Tonto.

When to Fish
Shore: Summer excellent, but hot. Spring and fall favored with cooler weather. Winter, with protection from north wind, can be excellent.
Inshore & offshore: Productive all year. April to August and October to Mid-November are best.

Accommodations & Services
La Paz, 45 minutes away, has all services, campgrounds, motels and five-star hotels. Meals and rooms in Las Arenas. Los Planes, off the highway, has markets, auto repair and camping.

Rating
Summer and fall this area rates an 8. In winter it drops to a 6.

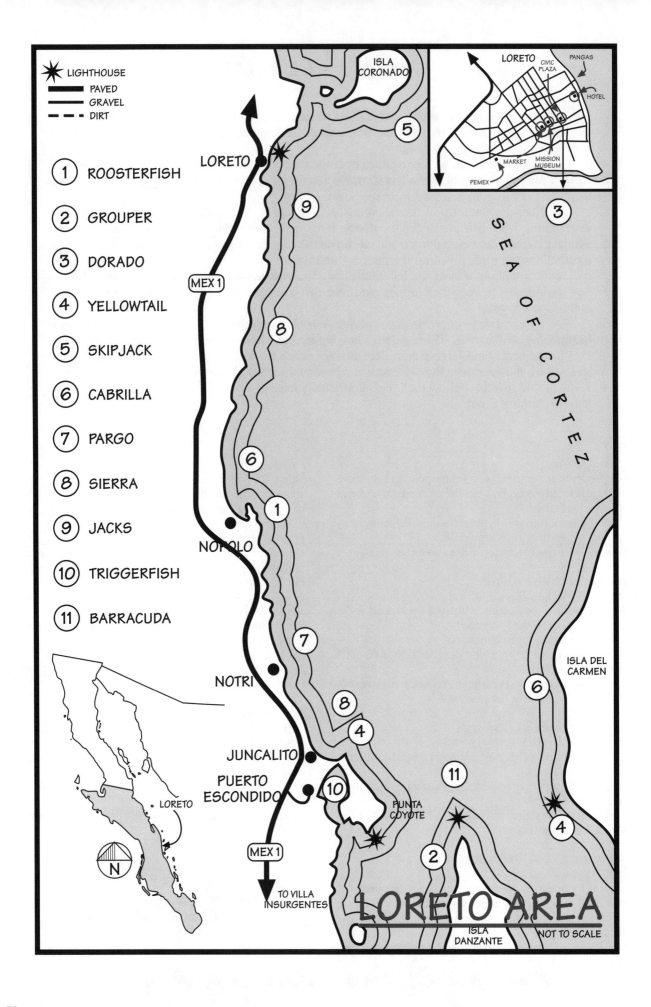

LIGHTHOUSE

━━━ PAVED
─── GRAVEL
--- DIRT

1 ROOSTERFISH
2 GROUPER
3 DORADO
4 YELLOWTAIL
5 SKIPJACK
6 CABRILLA
7 PARGO
8 SIERRA
9 JACKS
10 TRIGGERFISH
11 BARRACUDA

LORETO
PANGAS
CIVIC PLAZA
HOTEL
MARKET
MISSION MUSEUM
PEMEX

ISLA CORONADO
5
3
LORETO
9
MEX 1
SEA OF CORTEZ
8
6
1
NOPOLO
7
NOTRI
ISLA DEL CARMEN
8
4
6
11
JUNCALITO
PUERTO ESCONDIDO
10
PUNTA COYOTE
LORETO
2
4
N
MEX 1
TO VILLA INSURGENTES
ISLA DANZANTE

LORETO AREA
NOT TO SCALE

50

Loreto Area

*L*oreto's large panga fleet makes hiring a boat for your own fly fishing trip easy. Several companies here also offer inshore and offshore trips including Baja Bigfish Co. that caters to fly fishers. Beach areas south of Loreto are highlighted.

While in Loreto be sure to visit the Catholic Mission and the adjacent museum. Founded over 300 years ago by Jesuit Padre Juan María Salvatierra, it's the oldest mission in Baja. Loreto was also the original capital of Baja.

Loreto is fly rod-friendly beaches begin at Rancho Ligui, 20 miles (32 km) south. Take Mexico 1 and look for a dirt access road off to the left signed "Ligui." Take this to a small bay with a sandy beach protected by Isla Danzante to the east. Sardina baitfish here often get chased onto the beach by hungry jacks and roosterfish.

Four miles to the north of Ligui (off Mexico 1) is the turnoff for Puerto Escondido. A paved road leads to a pier at the entrance to a protected bay. Fly fish the bay from shore. Locals and visitors fish from the pier. My son likes to gaze into the clear water from the pier and pick out the fish he wants to catch. On the south side of the entrance road is the resort-like Tripui RV Park. Tripui offers rooms, a store, restaurant and RV parking.

A mile north of Puerto Escondido is Juncalito, the only area I've seen yellowtail caught from shore. Beaches are sand or pebbles with lots of structure. Heading up the road toward Loreto, notice the golf course. The big rock at Nopolo Cove, on the shoreline behind a green, is the next stop. Turn off at the sign for Eden Resort, bear right and go 1.5 miles (2 km).

This beach is a great place to spend the day. Walk to the big rock. Around its base are places where the water is 50' deep. With mask and snorkel lie on the flat portion of the rock to view fish. We have seen porpoises and other sea life swim up against the face of this 50' wall.

Types of Fish
Shore: Rock areas - cabrilla, grouper, triggerfish, pompano, croaker. Sandy areas - jacks, rooster, pompano, ladyfish, needlefish, sierra, pargo, corvina.
Inshore: Dorado, rooster, bonito, sierra, jacks, barracuda, triggerfish, cornet, needlefish.
Offshore: Dorado, sailfish, marlin, skipjack, yellowtail, yellowfin tuna.

Equipment to Use - Shore
Rods: 7 to 10 weight, 9'.
Line: Sandy areas - full fly line (350 grain) or shooting head. Rock areas - intermediate or floating with sink-tip.
Leaders: 20 lb. non-tapered mono, 6'.
Reels: Direct or anti-reverse for saltwater, disc drag, quick take-apart for cleaning.
Other: Polarized sunglasses, stripping basket, foot protection. Float tube or pontoon boat.

Equipment to Use - Inshore
Rods: 8 to 11 weight, 9'.
Line: Full fly line (450 grain), shooting head/intermediate.
Leaders: 20 lb., non-tapered mono, 6'. Short wire shock tippet for sierra.
Reels: Same as for shore fishing.
Other: Same as for shore.

Equipment to Use - Offshore
Rods: 10 to 12 weight, 8' - 9'. For billfish, 14 wt., quality reel, lots of backing. If not interested in I.G.F.A. rules use 125 lb., 36" bite tippet.

Line: Full fly line (650 grain), shooting head/intermediate.
Leaders: 20 lb. with shock tippet for billfish.
Reels: Same as inshore only larger.
Other: Butt plate for fighting big fish.

Flies to Use
Shore: 2/0 to 4/0, 1" - 4". Alf, Clouser, Bendback, white, gray, brown, blue or green Deceivers, sardina and smelt patterns tied with lots of flash. Blue, green, or white Popovics Surf Candy.
Inshore: Same flies as for shore.
Offshore: Large Alf, Clouser and streamers. For billfish - Tandem Deceivers, Bill & Kate Howe Big Game Fly, El Tonto.

When to Fish
Shore: Low light a.m. and p.m. Incoming tides produce best action. Midday for sight casting.
Inshore: Early morning and late afternoon.
Offshore: All day. At slack tide fish where you have seen the most fish that day.

Accommodations & Services
Camping is the main option in most of these areas, or return to Loreto. There are some services (store, food) at the Tripui RV Park. The closest gas station is in Loreto.

Rating
This area is a middle of the pack 5.

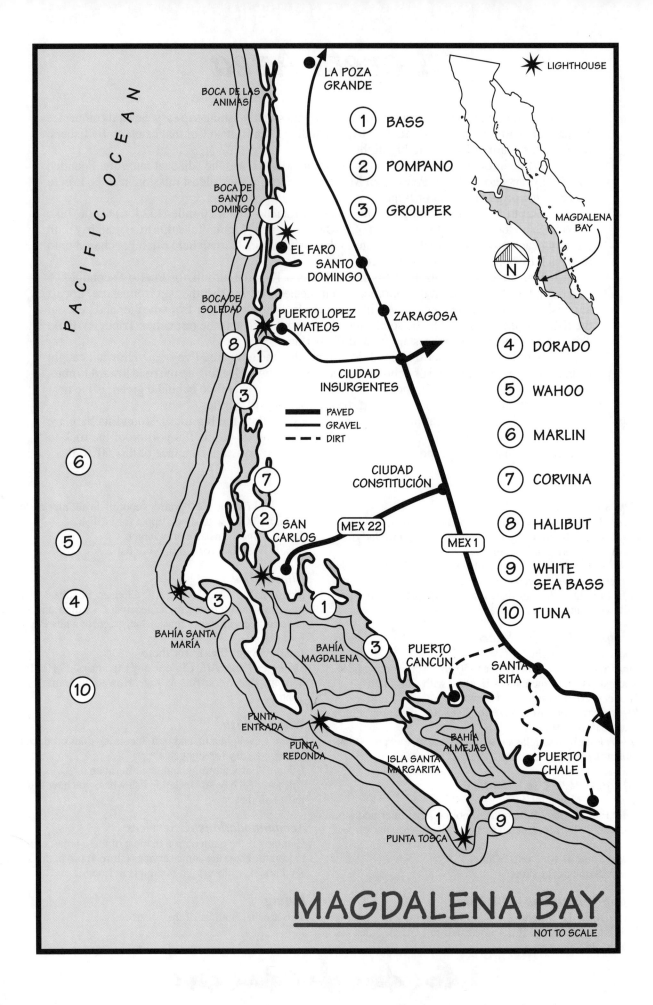

MAGDALENA BAY

NOT TO SCALE

Magdalena Bay

Mag Bay is the largest bay on the Baja peninsula, is on the Pacific side and is about 800 miles south of the U.S. border. Saltwater fly fishing here is like angling in fresh water for much larger fish. The bay, including Bahía Almejas and a 65 mile channel north to San Jorge, is over 125 miles long! It warrants a fly fishing guidebook of its own so this summary intends to give you enough to start the journey. For more information, pick up a copy of Gary Graham's *Fly Fishing Magdalena Bay*.

With mangrove trees surrounding most of the shoreline, shallower and warmer water, and almost everything else, Mag Bay is unique in Southern Baja. The mangroves require fly fishers to use pangas. Once in a boat you'll have numerous coves, back bays and deep channels to fish.

Hire pangas in the town of San Carlos. Motor 20 miles to the harbor entrance for a variety of gamefish. Farther outside is a series of high spots on the ocean floor — popular destinations for long-range fishing boats from Southern California.

In the bay's deep water along the western edge, one can have almost non-stop action with many gamefish. Let your fly sink, then put on the quick retrieve. Fish around the rocks with small brown, gray or blue Clousers. Look for porgy, cabrilla and pargo while exploring the down-current side of rocks.

On the sandy bottom areas try light blue, gray or green patterns up to 5". Mimic the common ballyhoo and sardina baitfish that get chased across the water by large fish.

Travel farther north to Puerto Lopez Mateos and you'll also need to hire a panga to fly fish. Fish where the current comes close to the mangroves. In winter this area is one of the better places to view the migrating California gray whales.

The area is accessed from paved roads off Mexico 1. San Carlos is about 34 miles (55 km) from the highway. The road to Lopez Mateos is about 24 miles (38 km) off Mexico 1 at Ciudad Insurgentes.

Types of Fish
Bay: Porgy, cabrilla, pargo, pompano, grouper, halibut.
Offshore: Marlin, sailfish, tuna, wahoo and dorado around high spots outside the bay in the blue water.

Equipment to Use - Bay
Rods: 8 to 10 weight, 9'.
Lines: Sandy areas - full fly line (350 grain) or shooting head. Intermediate or floating with sink-tip around mangroves.
Leaders: 20 lb. non-tapered mono, 6'. Wire tippet for sierra and barracuda.
Reels: Direct or anti-reverse, disc drag for saltwater, quick take-apart for cleaning.
Other: Polarized sunglasses, stripping basket.

Equipment to Use - Offshore
Rods: 10 to 14 weight, 8' - 9'.
Lines: Full fly line (650 grain) shooting head or intermediate. For billfish - 14 weight rod, quality reel, lots of backing. If not interested in I.G.F.A. rules use 125 lb. bite tippet, 36".
Leaders: 20 lb. with shock tippet for billfish.
Reels: Same as used in the bay.
Other: Polarized sunglasses, butt plate for big fish.

Flies to Use
Bay: 2/0 - 4/0 hook, 1" - 4", Alf, Clouser, Bendback, Deceiver in white, gray, brown, blue or green, sardina and smelt patterns. Use plenty of flash. Blue, green or white Popovics Surf Candy.
Offshore: Large Alf, Clouser and streamers. For billfish - Tandem Deceiver, Bill & Kate Howe Big Game Fly, El Tonto.

When to Fish
Bay: Low light a.m. and p.m. Incoming tides produce best action. Midday has the best sight casting opportunities.
Offshore: All day can be good. At slack tide, fish where you've seen the most fish that day.

Accommodations & Services
San Carlos and Puerto Lopez Mateos offer a full range of services including gasoline, hotels, restaurants and stores.

Rating
This area is different from other places in Southern Baja and rates a 7 for bay and offshore fly fishing.

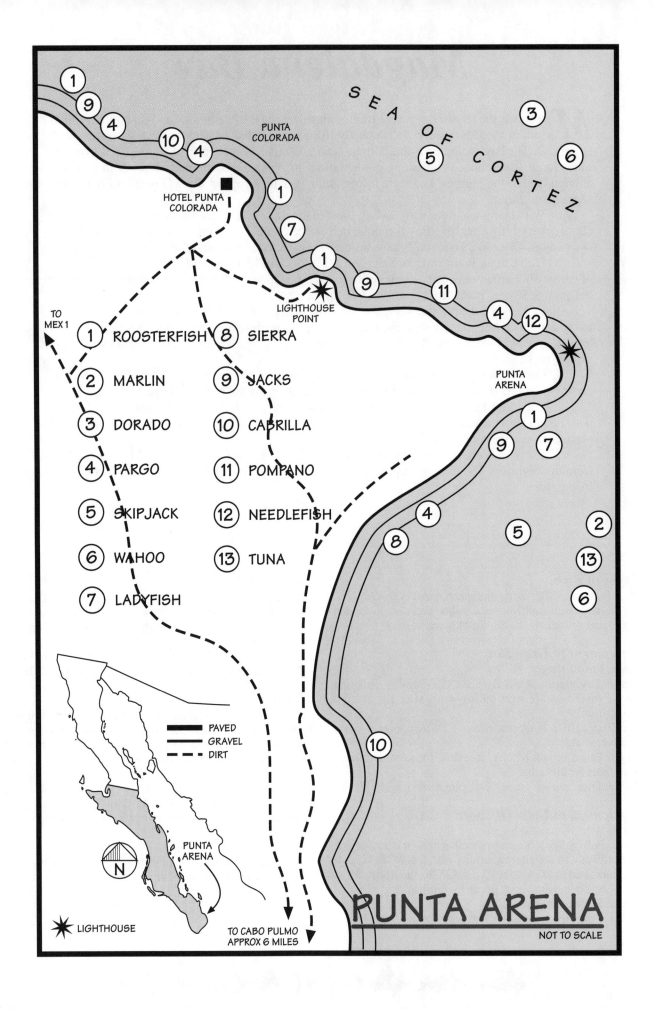

SEA OF CORTEZ

PUNTA COLORADA

HOTEL PUNTA COLORADA

LIGHTHOUSE POINT

PUNTA ARENA

TO MEX 1

1 ROOSTERFISH   8 SIERRA

2 MARLIN   9 JACKS

3 DORADO   10 CABRILLA

4 PARGO   11 POMPANO

5 SKIPJACK   12 NEEDLEFISH

6 WAHOO   13 TUNA

7 LADYFISH

PAVED
GRAVEL
DIRT

PUNTA ARENA

N

LIGHTHOUSE

TO CABO PULMO
APPROX 6 MILES

PUNTA ARENA

NOT TO SCALE

Punta Arena & Punta Colorada

*T*hese remote areas are for the more adventuresome and hardy fly fisher. We fly fish this area using 4 wheel ATVs for leg power and to get around some of the rocks. This area can offer the dedicated fly fisher many and diverse opportunities including sight casting to cruising fish or working the rocky structure.

Punta Colorada, one of the older hotels in the area, advertises as the roosterfish capital of Baja. There is plenty of fish structure in the shallow water in front of the hotel. A long sandy beach leads south to the lighthouse at Punta Arena. One can stay here, wake up in the morning, walk out to the water and start fishing.

Punta Arena, south of Punta Colorada, is unique as the 100 fathom curve comes within 1/8 of a mile of the beach. Large pompano, ladyfish, sierra, jacks, rooster and needlefish stack up against this color break. I've even seen rare dorado and wahoo within casting distance of shore.

An effective technique for these areas is fishing the down-current side of rocks. In the areas with sandy bottoms try 5" flies in light blue, gray or green. Ballyhoo, longer than the sardina, is a common baitfish in this area.

Access by going north from Los Cabos Airport on the highway Mexico 1. Take the turnoff at Las Cuevas and follow signs toward La Ribera. Just before this town look for a sign for Hotel Punta Colorada. Take this road, which is paved beyond Punta Colorada. Follow Punta Colorada signs at dirt roads for beach access. Another beach area is accessed by taking a right turn, just before the hotel entrance, and following signs to Lighthouse Point.

To reach Punta Arena continue a few miles farther on the road mentioned above and turn left on one of the dirt roads to get to the beach.

Types of Fish
Shore: Rock areas - cabrilla, pargo, triggerfish, pompano, croaker, etc. Sandy areas - jacks, roosterfish, pompano, ladyfish, giant needlefish, sierra, cornetfish.
Inshore: Dorado, wahoo, rooster, bonita, skipjack, sierra, jacks, pompano, triggerfish and giant needlefish along the color line.
Offshore: Marlin, sailfish, tuna, wahoo, dorado.

Equipment to Use - Shore
Rods: 7 to 10 weight, 9'.
Line: Sandy areas - full fly line (350 grain) or shooting head. Rock areas, intermediate or floating with sink-tip.
Leaders: 20 lb., non-tapered monofilament, 6'.
Reels: Direct or anti-reverse, disc drag for saltwater. Quick take-apart for cleaning.
Other: Stripping basket, foot protection for rocks. Float tube or pontoon boat if desired.

Equipment to Use - Inshore
Rods: 8 to 11 weight, 9'.
Line: Full fly line (450 grain) shooting head/intermediate.
Leaders: 20 lb. non-tapered mono, 6'. Short wire shock tippet for sierra and barracuda.
Reels: Same as for shore use.
Other: Float tube or small pontoon boat.

Equipment to Use - Offshore
Rods: 10 to 14 weight, 8' - 9'. For billfish, 14 weight rod.
Line: Full fly line (650 grain) shooting head/intermediate.
Leaders: 20 lb. with shock tippet for billfish. If not interested in I.G.F.A. rules, 125 lb. 36" bite tippet.
Reels: Same as for shore only larger.
Other: Butt plate for fighting big fish.

Flies to Use
Shore, inshore: 2/0 - 4/0, 1" - 4", Alf, Clouser, Bendback, Deceiver in white, gray, brown, blue or green, sardina and smelt patterns. Use plenty of flash. Also Popovics Surf Candy in blue, green and white. Small brown, gray or blue Clouser around rocks for croaker, pompano.
Offshore: Large Alf, Clouser and streamers. For billfish - Tandem Deceiver, Bill & Kate Howe Big Game Fly, El Tonto.

When to Fish
Shore: Low light a.m. and late p.m. Incoming tides produce best. Sight cast midday.
Inshore: Early morning and late afternoon.
Offshore: All day. At slack tide fish where you've seen the most fish that day.

Accommodations & Services
Best bet is the Hotel Punta Colorada. Beach camping or the hotels at Buena Vista to the north or Cabo Pulmo to the south. The town of Los Barriles has gas, stores, restaurants and other services.

Rating
This area is a strong 6 for shore, inshore and offshore fly fishing.

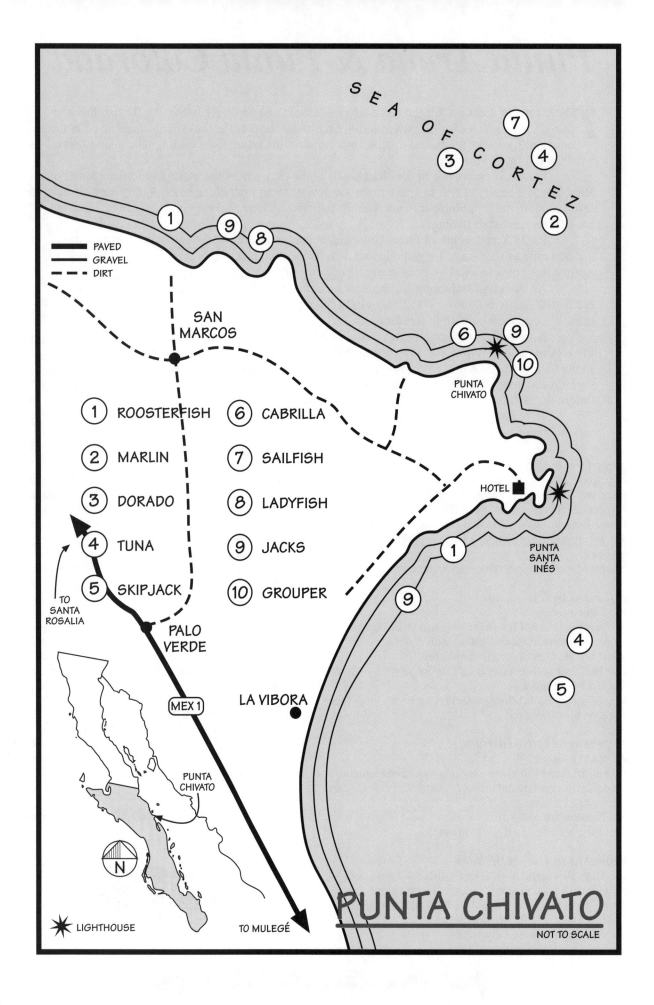

SEA OF CORTEZ

PAVED
GRAVEL
DIRT

SAN MARCOS

① ROOSTERFISH
② MARLIN
③ DORADO
④ TUNA
⑤ SKIPJACK

⑥ CABRILLA
⑦ SAILFISH
⑧ LADYFISH
⑨ JACKS
⑩ GROUPER

PUNTA CHIVATO

HOTEL

PUNTA SANTA INÉS

TO SANTA ROSALIA

PALO VERDE

MEX 1

LA VIBORA

PUNTA CHIVATO

N

LIGHTHOUSE

TO MULEGÉ

PUNTA CHIVATO

NOT TO SCALE

Punta Chivato

Punta Chivato is at the end of a 7.5 mile peninsula the juts into the middle of the Sea of Cortez near San Bruno. The peninsula offers three types of shore fly angling: rocky shoreline, sandy beach and areas full of various kinds of fish structure. There are limited boat launch and diving facilities in the area.

Three points, about 2 miles across, comprise the peninsula's tip. Hotel Punta Chivato, a boat ramp and campground are at the southernmost tip near Punta Santa Inés. Just before the hotel, look for a dirt road going to the north. This takes you to the northern side of the peninsula, which is mostly rocky shoreline holding a variety of resident fish. You'll find some sand dunes en-route to Punta Chivato, the northern point of the peninsula. Around the rocks fish for grouper and cabrilla with small Clouser flies in brown, gray, or blue. Remember, to be most effective fish the down-current side of the rocks.

The sandy beaches (from the hotel go south) offer great sight casting opportunities for rooster, jacks, sierra, grouper, cabrilla, etc. A common baitfish is sardina, so, on the sand, try bigger fly patterns (up to 5") in light blue, gray or green. Beyond the campground to the north there is plenty of structure to explore. Many times poppers are effective in this structure and over these sandy beaches.

Hotel Punta Chivato has a fleet of charter boats if you decide to take a trip offshore. The Hotel balcony is a great place to view what many consider to be the best sunsets in Baja.

Reach this area by driving on the Mexico 1 Highway. The turnoff has a sign and is near Palo Verde, approximately 13 miles (41 km) from Santa Rosalia or 12 miles (20 km) from Mulegé. The gravel-dirt road is approximately 12 miles long and leads you directly into Punta Chivato.

Types of Fish
Shore: Rooster, jacks, sierra, grouper, cabrilla.
Inshore: Dorado, yellowtail, rooster, spotted bay bass, grouper, bonito, sierra, jacks, barracuda, triggerfish, ladyfish.
Offshore: Dorado, marlin, sailfish, skipjack, giant needlefish, yellowtail and yellowfin tuna.

Equipment to Use - Shore
Rods: 7 to 10 weight, 9'.
Line: Sandy areas - full fly line (350 grain) or shooting head. Around rocks - intermediate or floating with sink-tip.
Leaders: 20 lb. non-tapered mono, 6'.
Reels: Direct or anti-reverse, disc drag for saltwater, quick take-apart for cleaning.
Other: Polarized sunglasses, stripping basket, foot protection from rocks. Float tube or pontoon boat.

Equipment to Use - Inshore
Rods: 8 to 11 weight, 9'.
Line: Full fly line (450 grain) shooting head/intermediate.
Leaders: 20 lb. non-tapered mono, 6'. Short wire shock tippet for sierra.
Reels: Same as for shore only larger.
Other: Same as for shore.

Equipment to Use - Offshore
Rods: 10 to 12 weight, 8' - 9'. For billfish, 14 weight, quality reel, lots of backing. If not interested in I.G.F.A. rules, try 125 lb., 36" bite tippet.
Line: Full fly line (650 grain) shooting head/intermediate.
Leaders: 20 lb. with shock tippet for billfish.
Reels: Same as for inshore only larger.
Other: Same as above, butt plate for fighting big fish.

Flies to Use
Shore: 2/0 - 4/0 hook, 1" - 4", Alf, Clouser, Bendback, white, gray, brown, blue and green Deceivers, sardina and smelt patterns. Use plenty of flash. Blue, green or white Popovics Surf Candy.
Inshore: Same as above.
Offshore: Large Alf, Clouser and streamers. For billfish - Tandem Deceivers, Bill & Kate Howe Big Game Fly, El Tonto with 6/0 hooks.

When to Fish
Shore: Low light a.m. and p.m. Incoming tides produce best action. Sight cast midday. Breezes usually start mid-morning, fish at morning gray light for best conditions.
Inshore: Early morning and late afternoon.
Offshore: All day can be good. At slack tide go where you've seen the most fish that day.

Accommodations & Services
Hotel Punta Chivato or the campgrounds if you want to spend the night. If day fishing, make headquarters in the town of Mulege, to the south or Santa Rosalia, to north.

Rating
This area is a middle of the pack 5 for beach, inshore and offshore fly fishing.

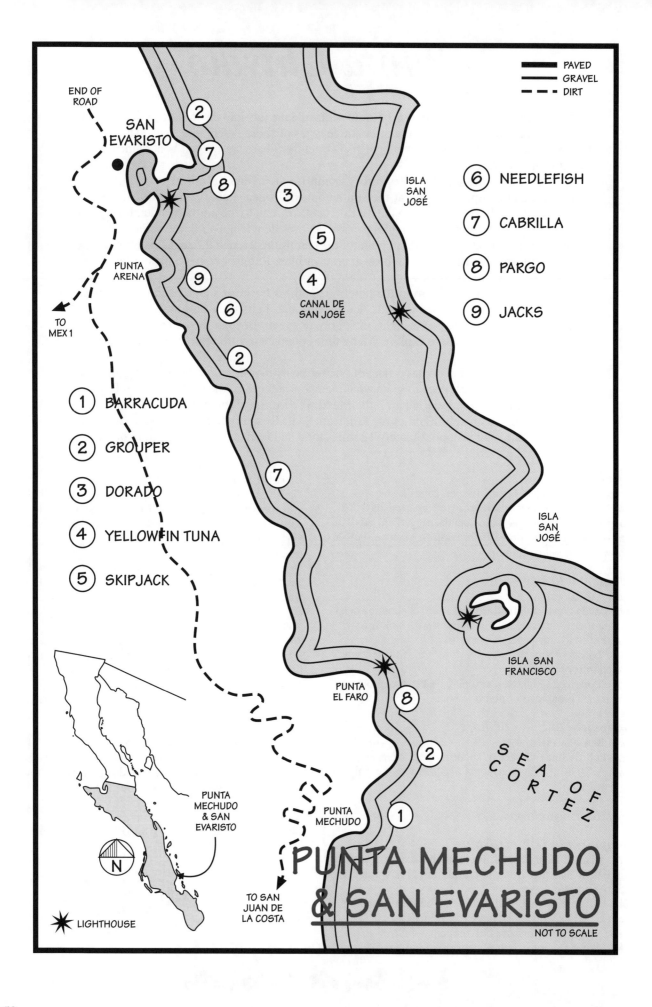

PAVED
GRAVEL
DIRT

END OF ROAD

SAN EVARISTO

ISLA SAN JOSÉ

⑥ NEEDLEFISH

⑦ CABRILLA

⑧ PARGO

⑨ JACKS

③

⑤

④

CANAL DE SAN JOSÉ

PUNTA ARENA

TO MEX 1

⑨

⑥

②

① BARRACUDA

② GROUPER

③ DORADO

④ YELLOWFIN TUNA

⑤ SKIPJACK

⑦

ISLA SAN JOSÉ

ISLA SAN FRANCISCO

PUNTA EL FARO

⑧

②

PUNTA MECHUDO & SAN EVARISTO

PUNTA MECHUDO

①

S E A   O F   C O R T E Z

PUNTA MECHUDO
& SAN EVARISTO

TO SAN JUAN DE LA COSTA

✦ LIGHTHOUSE

N

NOT TO SCALE

Punta Mechudo & San Evaristo

*I*f a remote fly fishing adventure is for you, these are your spots! On this trip you will drive, fish rocky areas, drive, fish beaches and drive some more. Here's how.

From La Paz, head north past the airport, to El Centenario and take the road to the right to San Juan de la Costa. Turn right on a graded dirt road at the northern end of San Juan de la Costa. Look for an "Evaristo 72 km" sign.

Going north you'll see a reef parallel to the beach. Often birds dive into bait balls of sardina and ballyhoo while barracuda and sierra break the surface. Tie on a wire bite tippet, baitfish imitation and cast into the white water caused by baitfish being chased by the feeding fish.

Farther along the road, notice the eerie effect of the phosphate rich soil: hills are shades of green and brown. Take the 10 miles of shore road to Punta Tarabillas. Scan the ocean for birds, bait and boiling fish indicating spots to fish. At Punta Coyote you can often hire someone, for a reasonable fee, to take you fishing with their skiff. Next, Punta Mechudo, has 3 points and offers different conditions. The intimidating but passable road climbs over the first point, doesn't require 4-wheel-drive and affords spectacular coastline views.

In the arroyo between the south and middle finger, a gravel beach has structure, a number of fishes and sea life. Before fishing, take your fins, mask and snorkel and survey. With this reconnaissance, pick a spot to fish. This is a fun reason you'll enjoy fly fishing Baja.

Drive over the next finger, the second beach is on the north side of the point. A sandy beach with rocky structure is to the south. Fish for cabrilla and pargo around the rocks.

North, toward Punta Arena (there's more than one in Baja), there are various types of shoreline. Fish one that looks promising. Near Punta Arena a small road comes in from Mexico 1. It's rough and not recommended!

Lastly, a few miles north at the small fishing village of San Evaristo, you can hire pangas to take you out to fish this small protected bay.

Types of Fish
Shore: Rock areas - cabrilla, pargo, triggerfish, pompano, grouper and croaker. Sandy areas - above fish plus jacks, roosterfish, ladyfish, giant needlefish, sierra, corvina.
Inshore: Above fish plus dorado, bonito, barracuda.
Offshore: Marlin, sailfish, tuna, wahoo, dorado between Punta Mechudo and Isla San Francisco.

Equipment to Use - Shore
Rods: 7 to 10 weight, 9'.
Line: Full fly line (350 grain) or shooting head for sandy areas. Intermediate or floating with sink-tip for rocks.
Leaders: 20 lb. non-tapered mono, 6'.
Reels: Direct or anti-reverse for saltwater, disc drag, quick take-apart for cleaning.
Other: Polarized sunglasses, stripping basket, foot protection, float tube or pontoon boat.

Equipment to Use - Inshore
Rods: 8 to 11 weight, 9'.
Line: Full fly line (450 grain) shooting head/intermediate.
Leaders: 20 lb. non-tapered mono, 6'. Use short wire shock tippet for sierra.
Reels/other: Same as for shore.

Equipment to Use - Offshore
Rods: 10 to 14 weight, 8' to 9'.
Line: Full fly line (650 grain) shooting head/intermediate. Billfish - 14 weight rod, quality reel, lots of backing. If not interested in I.G.F.A. rules, 125 lb., 36" bite tippet.

Leaders: 20 lb. with shock tippet for billfish.
Reels: Same as inshore only larger.
Other: Polarized sunglasses, butt plate for big fish.

Flies to Use
Shore: 2/0 to 4/0 hook, 1" to 4", Alf, Clouser, Bendback, Deceiver in white, gray, brown, blue or green. Sardina, smelt patterns. Use plenty of flash. Blue, green, or white Popovics Surf Candy.
Inshore: Same as those used from shore (above).
Offshore: Large Alf, Clouser and streamers. For billfish - Tandem Deceiver, Bill & Kate Howe Big Game Fly, El Tonto.

When to Fish
Shore: Low light a.m. and p.m. Incoming tides produce better action. Sight cast midday.
Inshore: Early morning and late afternoon.
Offshore: All day can be good. At slack tide, fish where you have seen the most fish that day.

Accommodations & Services
No services so beach camp, or return to La Paz. Closest gas is in La Paz. Some stores and services in El Centenario. In an emergency you might find some gas at the Mining Co. in San Juan de la Costa.

Rating
This area is a 6 for the shore and inshore. Offshore it's an 8.

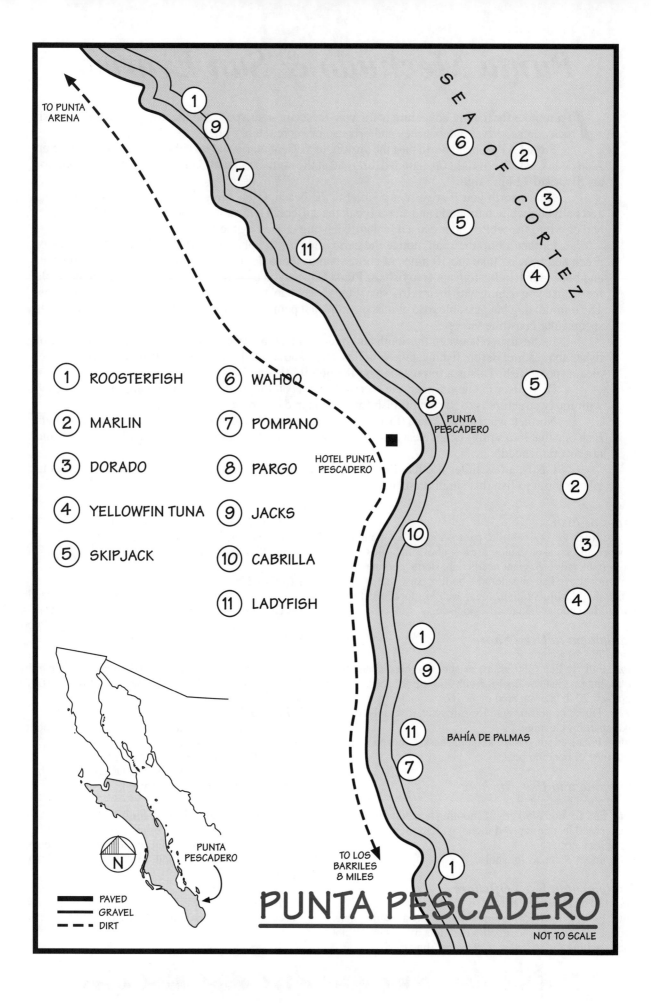

SEA OF CORTEZ

TO PUNTA
ARENA

1 ROOSTERFISH   6 WAHOO

2 MARLIN   7 POMPANO

3 DORADO   8 PARGO

4 YELLOWFIN TUNA   9 JACKS

5 SKIPJACK   10 CABRILLA

11 LADYFISH

HOTEL PUNTA
PESCADERO

PUNTA
PESCADERO

BAHÍA DE PALMAS

PUNTA
PESCADERO

N

TO LOS
BARRILES
8 MILES

PAVED
GRAVEL
DIRT

PUNTA PESCADERO

NOT TO SCALE

Punta Pescadero

*F*ly fishing in this area is a special treat reminiscent of fishing a rocky river bank, except you and the water are warm! This point offers a lot of exposed structure that provides cover for a myriad of fish ready to take a well-presented offering. Pinpoint casts and quick retrieves will produce rod-rattling strikes that take your breath away.

You will find more rocky shore than sandy beaches here. The rocky beaches are covered with stones from marble to basketball size that makes for difficult walking. The only access road to Punta Pescadero is dirt and sometimes requires a high clearance or 4-wheel-drive vehicle.

To reach the Pescadero area, drive through the town of Los Barriles and take the dirt road on the west side of town. Drive approximately 8 miles (14 km) to Punta Pescadero. Along the way are various roads that access the shoreline. As the road climbs the mountain side the views become spectacular.

Types of Fish
Shore: Cabrilla, grouper, pargo, triggerfish, other species may breeze through.
Inshore: Dorado, roosterfish, bonito, skipjack, sierra, jacks, pompano, triggerfish, giant needlefish.
Offshore: Marlin, sailfish, tuna, wahoo, dorado.

Equipment to Use - Shore
Rods: 7 to 10 weight, 9'.
Line: Intermediate or floating, sink-tip for around the rocks. Also use intermediate on the few sandy beaches.
Leaders: 20 lb. non-tapered mono, 6'.
Reels: Direct or anti-reverse, disc drag for saltwater, quick take-apart for cleaning.
Other: Polarized sunglasses, stripping basket, foot protection from rocks. Float tube or pontoon boat.

Equipment to Use - Inshore
Rods: 8 to 11 weight, 9'.
Line: Full fly line (450 grain) shooting head/intermediate.
Leaders: 20 lb. non-tapered mono, 6'. Short wire shock tippet for sierra.
Reels: Same as for shore.
Other: Same as shore equipment.

Equipment to Use - Offshore
Rods: 10 to 14 weight, 8' - 9'.
Line: Full fly line (650 grain) shooting head/intermediate.
Leaders: 20 lb. with shock tippet for billfish.
Reels: Same as for inshore only bigger and stronger.
Other: Polarized sunglasses, butt plate for fighting big ones.

Flies to Use
Shore: 2/0 to 4/0, 1" - 4", Clouser, Deceiver, Alf, in white, gray, brown, blues or green, sardina, smelt. Use plenty of flash. Blue, green or white Popovics Surf Candy, sand eel in baitfish colors.
Inshore: Same as above but no eels.
Offshore: Same as above, plus heavy Clousers (#7 hook). For billfish - Tandem Deceiver, Bill & Kate Howe Big Game Fly, El Tonto.

When to Fish
Shore: Winter, offers protection from north wind. Early Spring to Fall great, skip the September chubasco (hurricane) time. I prefer early a.m. first, late p.m. second.
Inshore & offshore: Year around. April to August and October to Mid-November best. At slack tide fish where you have seen the most fish that day.

Accommodations & Services
Los Barriles has a full range of hotels, bungalows and houses for rent several markets, a hardware store and, down the road at Buena Vista, a gas station. The Punta Pescadero Hotel, at the other end of the road, is reliable but there are no other services.

Rating
This area is a solid 5 for year around fly fishing, during peak times of the year a 7.

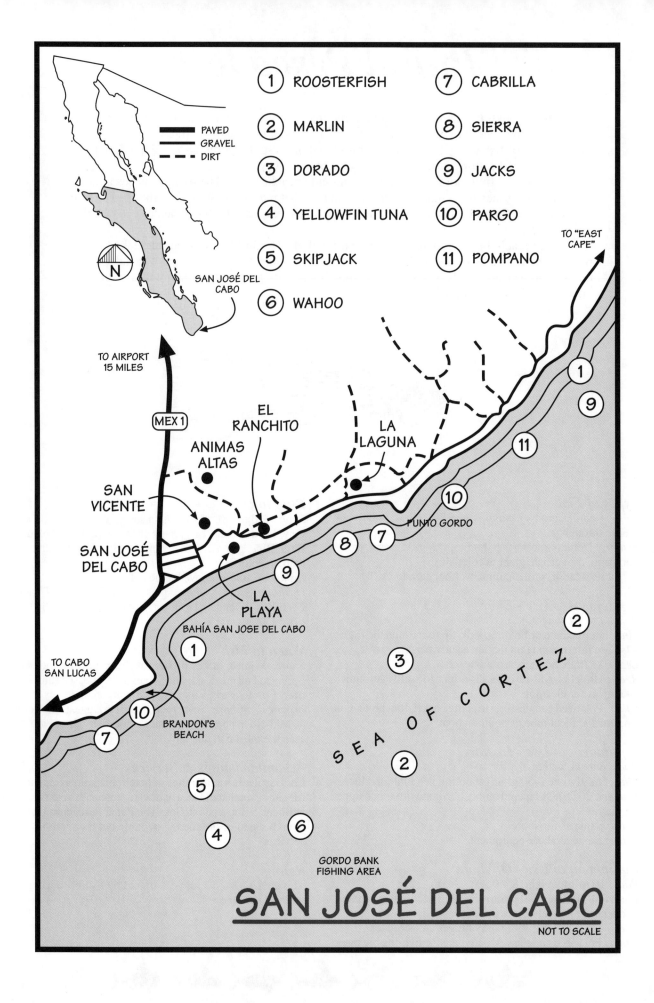

SAN JOSÉ DEL CABO

NOT TO SCALE

San José del Cabo
East Cape Loop

*I*t's surprising how little pressure this area receives considering the easy access. This can be a great road trip for the fly angler: vistas, beaches and bumpy dirt roads. Don't let the dust deter you from the secluded beaches awaiting your exploration.

From the Los Cabos airport, take Mexico 1 south about 30 km (19 miles) towards San José Del Cabo. Turn left on Calle Canseco to Boulevard Mijares. Turn left to Calle Juarez and take the dirt road signed to La Playita. The village is after the National Park Bird Sanctuary.

La Playita has pangas for rent which afford quick access to the Gordo Banks fish zone. Wahoo fishing can be extraordinary January to May, usually during the first 2 hours of daylight.

The road around the village goes up coast to Los Frailes. North of La Playita is populated but there aren't any stores until La Ribera. La Playita is the last place to stock up on snacks, water, etc. If you are on a multi-day outing carry camping gear, food and water. The first hotel you come across, heading up coast, is Los Frailes. At Vinorama a westbound road provides a "shortcut" back to the Los Cabos airport.

Beach fishing the "loop" stretch can be very good for jacks, cabrilla, roosterfish, sierra and many other species. Around the rocks you will often find feeding porgy, cabrilla, pargo, and pompano. Try fishing the down-current side of the rocks using small brown, gray or blue Clousers. On the sand, try bigger patterns (up to 5") in light blue, gray or green. Ballyhoo and sardina are the predominate baitfish in this area. Watch for ballyhoo being chased across the water by larger fish. This is your clue as to where to cast your fly.

East Cape shores are influenced by the Pacific Ocean. Large swells are common and a number of beaches have excellent surfing. Wading anglers should use caution and watch for big waves, swells and undertow. On many beaches a float tube or pontoon is too risky.

Types of Fish
Shore: Rock areas - cabrilla, pargo, triggerfish, pompano, croaker, jacks, rooster, pompano, ladyfish, needlefish, sierra.
Inshore: Dorado, wahoo, roosterfish, bonita, skipjack, sierra, jacks, pompano, triggerfish, needlefish.
Offshore: Marlin, sailfish, tuna, wahoo, dorado.

Equipment to Use - Shore
Rods: 8 to 10 weight, 9'.
Line: Full fly line (350 grain) or shooting head. Intermediate or floating with sink-tip for around rocks.
Leaders: 20 lb. non-tapered mono, 6'.
Reels: Direct or anti-reverse, disc drag for saltwater, quick take-apart for cleaning.
Other: Polarized sunglasses, stripping basket, foot protection from rocks.

Equipment to Use - Inshore
Rods: 8 to 11 weight, 9'.
Line: Full fly line (450 grain), shooting head/intermediate.
Leaders: 20 lb. non-tapered mono, 6'. Use a short wire shock tippet for sierra.
Reels/Other: Same as for shore.

Equipment to Use - Offshore
Rods: 10 to 14 weight, 8' - 9'.
Line: Full fly line (650 grain) shooting head or intermediate. For billfish - 14 wt. rod, quality reel, lots of backing. If not interested in I.G.F.A. rules, 125 lb., 36" bite tippet.
Leaders: 20 lb. shock tippet for billfish.

Reels: Same as for inshore only larger.
Other: Polarized sunglasses, butt plate for big fish.

Flies to Use
Shore: 2/0 - 4/0 hook, 1" - 4", Clouser, Bendback, Deceiver, Alf, in white, gray, brown, blue or green. Sardina, smelt patterns. Tie plenty of flash. Blue, green, or white Popovics Surf Candy.
Inshore: Same as used from shore (above).
Offshore: Same as shore plus large streamers. For billfish - 6/0 hook, Tandem Deceiver, Bill & Kate Howe Big Game Fly, El Tonto.

When to Fish
Shore: Low light a.m. and p.m. Incoming tides produce best action. Sight cast midday.
Inshore: Early morning and late afternoon.
Offshore: All day can be good. At slack tide try to fish where you have seen the most fish that day.

Accommodations & Services
San José Del Cabo has a complete array of services. La Playita is the last place for lodging and supplies before you travel up the road to Los Frailes.

Rating
This area is a 6 for the shore and inshore, a 7 for offshore.

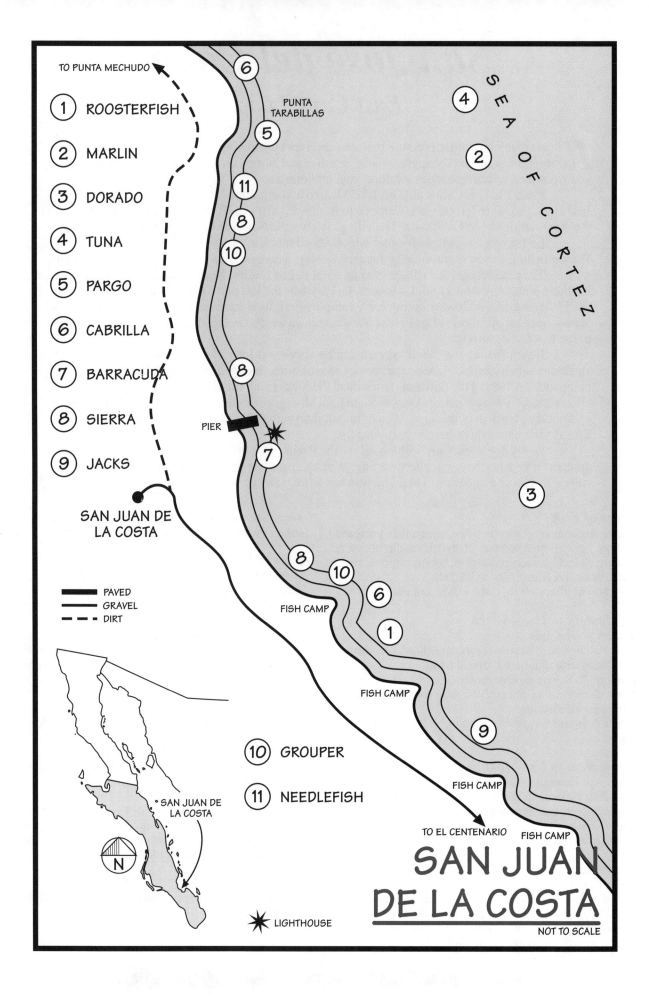

TO PUNTA MECHUDO

1 ROOSTERFISH

2 MARLIN

3 DORADO

4 TUNA

5 PARGO

6 CABRILLA

7 BARRACUDA

8 SIERRA

9 JACKS

SAN JUAN DE
LA COSTA

PAVED
GRAVEL
DIRT

10 GROUPER

11 NEEDLEFISH

PUNTA
TARABILLAS

SEA OF CORTEZ

PIER

FISH CAMP

FISH CAMP

FISH CAMP

FISH CAMP

TO EL CENTENARIO

SAN JUAN DE LA COSTA

SAN JUAN
DE LA COSTA

NOT TO SCALE

LIGHTHOUSE

N

SAN JUAN DE LA COSTA

San Juan de la Costa

*T*he area around this company-owned phosphate mining town offers fly fishing on sandy beaches, rocky shores and rock reefs. If staying in or around La Paz, a 35 mile (56 km) junket northwest leads to a great place to spend a day with a fly rod. The directions below are from La Paz and start you on your way fly fishing.

Travel north from La Paz on Mexico Highway 1 for about 10 miles (16 km). Spot a paved road going off to the right, signed "San Juan de la Costa and San Evaristo." Take this road, and counting arroyos, head to the 5th arroyo. This is just before you reach San Juan de la Costa, approximately 25 miles (40 km) north of the turnoff on Mexico 1.

From here, start working your way back down the entire area (south). All 5 arroyos have flat dirt points that extend from shore with clear water over sandy bottoms. Occasional dark patches indicate rock structure. Cast in each point area until you find some action.

This action can be cabrilla and pargo feeding in the rocks. Cast small brown, gray or blue Clousers in the down-current side of the rocks. In the sandy bottom areas use light blue, gray or green patterns 1" - 5". This will mimic sardina and ballyhoo, the common baitfish in these areas.

Approximately 5 miles before the turn-off back onto Mexico 1, on the east side of the road, is a graded dirt road (less than 1 mile long). Look for the sign for "Brisamar." This leads to a deserted beach that has some rock structure. Cast around the rocks and look for frigate birds diving on bait schools. If you see this activity, cast your fly in their direction.

Types of Fish
Shore: Rock areas - cabrilla, pargo, triggerfish, pompano, croaker. Sandy areas - jacks, roosterfish, pompano, ladyfish, needlefish, sierra, pargo, corvina.
Inshore: Rooster, bonito, sierra, jacks, barracuda, triggerfish, needlefish.
Offshore: Marlin, sailfish, tuna, wahoo, dorado outside the islands.

Equipment to Use - Shore
Rods: 7 to 10 weight, 9'.
Line: Sandy areas - full fly line (350 grain) or shooting head. Rock areas, intermediate or floating with sink-tip.
Leaders: 20 lb. non-tapered mono, 6'.
Reels: Direct or anti-reverse, disc drag for saltwater, quick take-apart for cleaning.
Other: Polarized sunglasses, stripping basket, foot protection from rocks. Float tube or pontoon boat.

Equipment to Use - Inshore
Rods: 8 to 11 weight, 9'.
Line: Full fly line (450 grain) shooting head system or intermediate.
Leaders: 20 lb. non-tapered mono, 6'. Short wire shock tippet for sierra.
Reels / Other: Same as for shore use.

Equipment to Use - Offshore
Rods: 10 to 14 weight, 8' - 9'.
Line: Full fly line (650 grain) shooting head/intermediate. For billfish - 14 wt. rod, quality reel, lots of backing. If not interested in I.G.F.A. rules tie on 36" bite tippet of 125 lbs.
Leaders: 20 lb. with shock tippet for billfish.
Reels: Same as for inshore only larger.
Other: Polarized sunglasses, butt plate for fighting big fish.

Flies to Use
Shore: 2/0 to 4/0, 1" - 4", Alf, Clouser, Bendback, Deceiver in white, gray, brown, blue or green. Sardina, smelt patterns. Tie on lots of flash. Blue, green, white Popovics Surf Candy.
Inshore: Same flies as used from shore.
Offshore: Beyond the islands: 7/0 hook, 8" - 10", Alf, Clouser and large streamers. For billfish - Tandem Deceiver, Bill & Kate Howe Big Game Fly, El Tonto.

When to Fish
Shore: Low light a.m. and p.m. Incoming tides produce better action. Sight cast midday.
Inshore: Early morning and late afternoon.
Offshore: Beyond the islands: All day can be good. At slack tide try to fish where you have seen the most fish that day.

Accommodations & Services
Camping only in San Juan de la Costa. No services. Return to La Paz for everything, including gas.

Rating
This area is a 4 for the shore and inshore fly fishing. Offshore, outside the islands, is a 7.

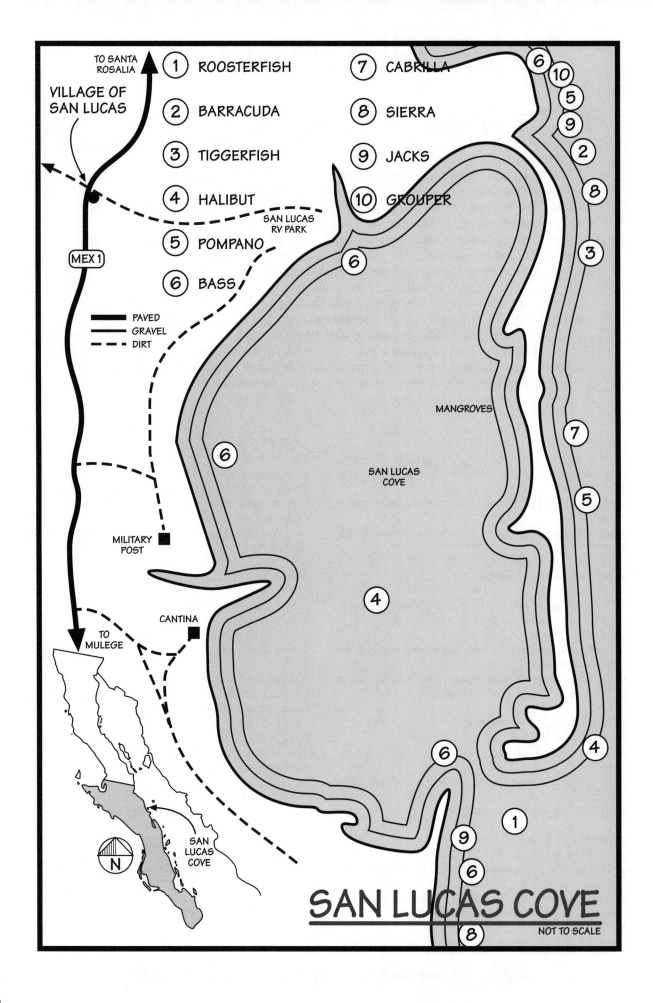

TO SANTA
ROSALIA

VILLAGE OF
SAN LUCAS

MEX 1

① ROOSTERFISH
② BARRACUDA
③ TIGGERFISH
④ HALIBUT
⑤ POMPANO
⑥ BASS

⑦ CABRILLA
⑧ SIERRA
⑨ JACKS
⑩ GROUPER

SAN LUCAS
RV PARK

━━━ PAVED
——— GRAVEL
- - - DIRT

MILITARY
POST

CANTINA

TO
MULEGE

SAN
LUCAS
COVE

N

MANGROVES

SAN LUCAS
COVE

SAN LUCAS COVE

NOT TO SCALE

San Lucas Cove

Caleta San Lucas

*C*aleta is Spanish meaning "little cove." The well-known San Lucas Cove has a very productive 1 mile wide by 2 mile long shoreline for fly anglers. The shore is complete with mangrove lined flats and gravel and sandy beaches. The caleta is protected by a rocky bar that can also be a good place to cast. The campground and the San Lucas RV Park are popular stopping-off places for all kinds of Baja travelers. These people, especially those returning from the south, can be great sources of fishing information and conditions farther down the peninsula.

The shoreline, both inside and outside the cove, offers ample fly rod opportunities for cabrilla, grouper, spotted bay bass, roosterfish, pompano and a variety of other species.

The entrance to the cove is also a popular fishing area outside. Depths reach 1,000' (305 meters) and nutrient-rich currents attract a noteworthy variety of gamefish to the area. These fish are especially south of Isla San Marcos and between the island and shore.

Offshore 4 miles is Isla San Marcos, where you can often see large ships taking on cargo at the mining operation on the south end of the island. Craig Channel extends 5 miles north and south between the island and shore and is home to the large fish for which Baja is renowned.

To get to San Lucas Cove, drive 10 miles (16 km) south of Santa Rosalia to San Lucas. A short distance off Mexico 1, look for a sign to "San Lucas RV Park" that takes you to the heart of the cove. Farther south on Mexico 1 at KM 180 (near the airstrip) is another road into the cove and the welcome shade of the palm-covered campgrounds.

Types of Fish
Shore: Rock areas - cabrilla, grouper, triggerfish, spotted bay bass, pompano, croaker. Sandy areas - cabrilla, jacks, roosterfish, pompano, ladyfish, giant needlefish, sierra, pargo, halibut.
Inshore: Dorado, yellowtail, rooster, spotted bay bass, grouper, bonito, sierra, jacks, barracuda, triggerfish, lizardfish.
Offshore: Dorado, sailfish, skipjack, yellowtail and yellowfin tuna.

Equipment to Use - Shore
Rods: 7 to 10 weight, 9'.
Line: Full fly line (350 grain) or shooting head. Intermediate or floating with sink-tip for around rocks.
Leaders: 20 lb. non-tapered mono, 6'.
Reels: Direct or anti-reverse for saltwater, disc drag, quick take-apart for cleaning.
Other: Polarized sunglasses, stripping basket, foot protection from rocks. Float tube or pontoon boat. No-see-ums and mosquitoes in this area, bring bug repellent.

Equipment to Use - Inshore
Rods: 8 to 11 weight, 9'.
Line: Full fly line (450 grain) shooting head/intermediate.
Leaders: 20 lb., non-tapered mono, 6'. Short wire shock tippet for sierra, barracuda.
Reels/Other: Same as for shore use.

Equipment to Use - Offshore
Rods: 10 to 12 weight, 8' - 9'. For billfish - 14 wt. rod, quality reel, lots of backing. If not interested in I.G.F.A. rules tie on 36" bite tippet of 125 lbs.
Line: Full fly line (650 grain) shooting head/intermediate.
Leaders: 20 lb. with shock tippet for billfish.
Reels: Same as for inshore only larger.
Other: Polarized sunglasses, butt plate for fighting big fish.

Flies to Use
Shore: 2/0 to 4/0, 1" - 4", Alf, Clouser, Bendback, Deceiver in white, gray, brown, blue or green. Sardina, smelt patterns. Tie on lots of flash. Popovics Surf Candy in blue, green or white.
Inshore: Same flies as used from shore.
Offshore: 6/0, 7" - 10", Alf, Clouser and streamers. Billfish, Tandem Deceiver, Bill & Kate Howe Big Game Fly, El Tonto.

When to Fish
Shore: Low light a.m. and p.m. Incoming tides produce best action. Sight cast midday.
Inshore: Early morning and late afternoon.
Offshore: All day can be good. At slack tide try to fish where you have seen the most fish that day.

Accommodations & Services
San Lucas has RV park, campgrounds a boat ramp and, as of this writing a small restaurant. Santa Rosalia offers a full range of services including gas. Be sure to visit the "French" bakery for their famous *bolillos*.

Rating
This area is a 4 for the shore and inshore. Offshore is a 5.

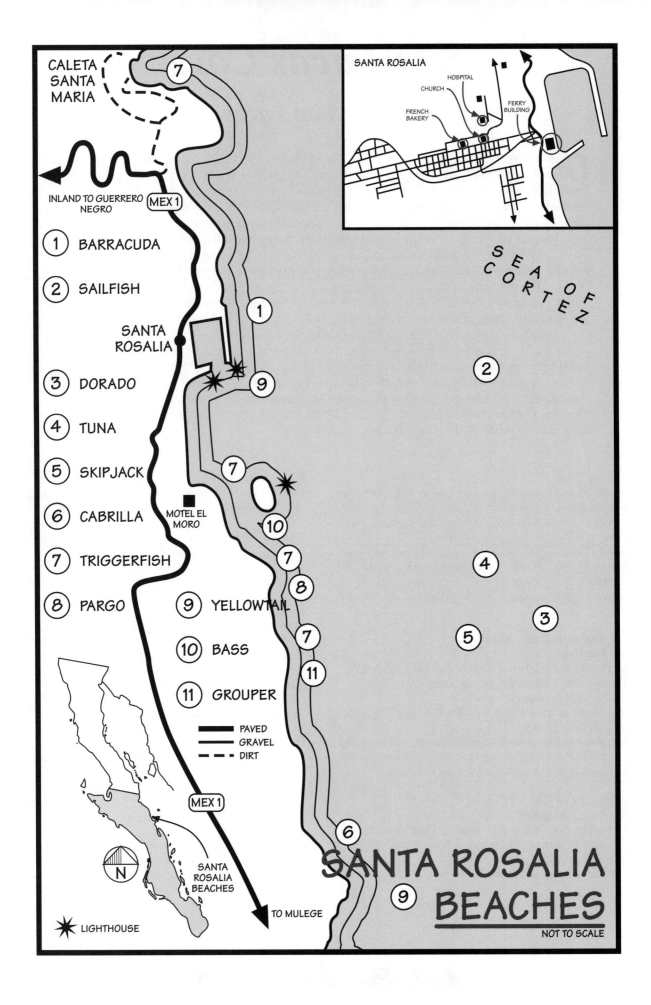

CALETA
SANTA
MARIA

INLAND TO GUERRERO
NEGRO   MEX 1

SANTA ROSALIA

CHURCH   HOSPITAL

FRENCH
BAKERY   FERRY
BUILDING

S E A
O F
C O R T E Z

① BARRACUDA

② SAILFISH

SANTA
ROSALIA

③ DORADO

④ TUNA

⑤ SKIPJACK

⑥ CABRILLA

MOTEL EL
MORO

⑦ TRIGGERFISH

⑧ PARGO

⑨ YELLOWTAIL

⑩ BASS

⑪ GROUPER

PAVED
GRAVEL
DIRT

MEX 1

N

SANTA
ROSALIA
BEACHES

TO MULEGE

★ LIGHTHOUSE

SANTA ROSALIA
BEACHES

NOT TO SCALE

Santa Rosalia Beaches

*T*he old mining town of Santa Rosalia looks exactly as you would expect — dust and dirt everywhere and surrounded by huge slag heaps — but with some surprises. The metal catholic church was designed by Alexandre Eiffel, of Eiffel Tower fame. It was assembled in Paris, taken apart, shipped by boat to Santa Rosalia, then reassembled.

The French company that started the mining company left other Parisian marks. The bakery serves a Mexican version of the French roll "bolillos" and the French influenced wooden architecture is as if you are in some type of strange New Orleans replica built by the Mexicans.

Santa Rosalia has several sport fishing operations. The small marina and the fishless beaches in town make fly rodders go a few miles north or south.

To the north, just before Mexico 1 turns up into the mountains, look for an abandoned dirt runway. Take the dirt road along the runway heading north. After about 1.5 miles the road bears left toward a guard shack and gate. Take the dirt road to the right. This road parallels the shore 3 miles to Campo Pesquero, a fish camp at the southern edge of Caleta Santa Maria.

Campo Pesquero is usually deserted weekends, but at certain times of the year mid-week can be busy. You can set up camp here or stay at one of the hotels in town. The north end of this bay has a large complex with noise, dust, buildings, a large pier and other things associated with mining.

Fishing along the Caleta Santa Maria bay shoreline can produce good action. The rocky point has grouper and other gamefish. You can hire one of the pangas for a day of inshore or offshore fishing.

To the south of Santa Rosalia, past the ferry and beyond the bus depot, the shoreline is rocky and can yield an assortment of fish. El Morro, a hotel on the bluff at the south end of town, is a good landmark. On the south side of the hotel there is more accessible shoreline until Mexico 1 turns back inland.

Types of Fish
Shore: Rocky point (north) - spotted bay bass, cabrilla, grouper, pargo, triggerfish. Sandy areas (south) - roosterfish, jacks, ladyfish, needlefish, pompano, sierra.
Inshore: Dorado, rooster, bonito, skipjack, sierra, jacks, pompano, triggerfish, needlefish, yellowtail.
Offshore: Yellowtail, barracuda, skipjack, dorado, needlefish.

Equipment to Use - Shore
Rods: 7 to 10 weight, 9'.
Line: Intermediate or floating with sink-tip for around the rocks. Intermediate also on sandy beaches.
Leaders: 20 lb. non-tapered mono, 6'.
Reels: Direct or anti-reverse, disc drag for saltwater, quick take-apart for cleaning.
Other: Polarized sunglasses, stripping basket and foot protection from rocks. Float tube or pontoon boat.

Equipment to Use - Inshore
Rods: 8 to 11 weight, 9'.
Line: Full fly line (450 grain) shooting head or intermediate.
Leaders: 20 lb. non-tapered mono, 6'. Short wire shock tippet for sierra.
Reels: Same as for shore.
Other: Polarized sunglasses, float tube or small inflatable pontoon boat.

Equipment to Use - Offshore
Rods: 10 to 12 weight, 8' to 9'.
Line: Full fly line (650 grain), shooting head/intermediate.
Leaders: 20 lb. with shock tippet for billfish.
Reels: Same as for inshore only larger.
Other: Polarized sunglasses, butt plate for big fish.

Flies to Use
Shore: 2/0 to 4/0, 1" - 4", Clouser, Deceiver, Alf, in white, gray, brown, blue or green. Sardina, smelt patterns. Tie on plenty of flash. Blue, green, or white Popovics Surf Candy. Sand eel in baitfish colors.
Inshore: Same as used from shore (above).
Offshore: Same as used inshore (above). Billfish, Tandem Deceiver, Bill & Kate Howe Big Game Fly, El Tonto.

When to Fish
Shore: Great fishing summertime. Spring and fall favored because of cooler weather. Winter, with protection from North wind, can have excellent fishing.
Inshore: Summer and late fall.
Offshore: April - August and October - mid-November.

Accommodations & Services
Santa Rosalia has all supplies and services you'll need.

Rating
Summer and fall rate a 6. Winter is a 3.

Roosterfish

Appendix

Spanish for The Southern Baja Fly Angler

*As a rule, Mexicans are very polite people. Most will treat you
with respect and tolerance, especially if you try to speak some of their language.*

Basic Vocabulary

Hello
Hola
(OH-la)

Good Bye
Adios
(Ah-dee-OHSS)

Good Morning
Buenos Días
(boo-EH-nos DEE-as)

Good Afternoon
Buenas Tardes
(boo-EH-nas TAR-des)

Good Night
Buenas Noches
(boo-EH-nas NO-ches)

How?
¿Cómo?
(KOH-moh)

How many?
¿Cuántos?
(KWAN-tohs)

How much?
¿Cuánto?
(KWAHN-toh)

Please
Por Favor
(por-fah-VOR)

Thank You
Gracias
(GRA-see-us)

Excuse me
Dispenseme
(des-PEN-sah-may)

Mister
Señor
(sen-YOR)

Lady
Señora
(sen-YOR-ah)

More
Más
(mahs)

Say it again
¿Mande?
(MAHN-day)

There
Allí
(ah-YEE)

This
Este
(ES-te)

That
Ese
(ES-eh)

Understand?
¿Comprende?
(kohm-PREHN-day)

Very
Muy
(MOO-ee)

Water
Agua
(AH-gwah)

Why?
¿Por qué?
(Pohr QUE?)

Yes
Sí
(see)

Vocabulary For Fly Fishing

Backwards
Reversa
(Ree-VER-sah)

Bandage
Venda
(VEN-dah)

Beach
Playa
(PLY-yah)

Bait
Carnada
(kahr-NA-da)

Beer
Cerveza
(sehr-Vey-sah)

Big
Grande
(GRAHN-day)

Birds
Pájaros
(PAH-ha-ros)

Bobbers
Velata
(ve-LAY-tah)

Boat
Lancha
(LAHN-chah)

Bucket
Cubo
(Coo-bo)

Clean
Limpiar
(lim-PYAR)

Cold
Frío
(FREE-oh)

East
Este
(ESS-te)

Empty
Vacío
(BA-cee-oh)

Faster
Rápido
(RAH-pe-doh)

Feather
Pluma
(PLOO-mah)

Fish
Pescado
(Pes-KA-doh)

Fly
Mosca
(Moska)

Forward
Adelante
(ah-dah-LAHN-tay)

Full
Lleno
(YEA-noh)

Gaff
Gancho
(GAHN-choh)

Here
Aquí
(ah-KEY)

Hot
Caliente
(kah-lee-EN-teh)

Ice
Hielo
(YEA-loh)

Is it far?
¿Está lejos?
(ES-tah LAY-hos)

Is it close?
¿Está cerca?
(ES-tah SEHR-kah)

Later
Más tarde
(mahs TAHR-day)

Left (turn)
Izquierda
(is-key-AIR-dah)

Less
Menos
(MAY-nos)

Line
Línea
(LEEN-eyah)

Little
Poco
(POH-koh)

Motor
Motor
(mo-TOR)

Mouth
Boca
(BO-cah)

Needle
Aguja
(ah-GOO-hah)

North
Norte
(NOR-tay)

Now
Ahora
(ah-O-rah)

Oars
Remos
(RAY-mos)

Opener
Abridor
(Ah-bre-DOR)

Panga
Panga
(PAHN-gah)

Please
Por favor
(Por-fah-VOR)

Pliers
Pinzas
(PIN-zas)

Rod
Caña
(KAHN-yah)

Reel
Carrete
(kah-RHET-tay)

Right (agree)
Correcto
(kor-REK-toh)

Right (turn)
Derecho
(deh-REH-choh)

Seasick
Mareado
(mah-day-AH-doh)

Slower
Despacio
(dehs-PAH-see-oh)

Small
Pequeño
(pay-KAIN-yoh)

South
Sur
(soor)

West
Oeste
(oh-ESS-tay)

Wind
Viento
(BEE-ehn-toh)

Phrases for Fly Fishing

I'm looking for
Busco
(BOO-scoh)

Look
Mira
(MEE-dah)

Don't touch
No toca
(No TOH-kah)

Don't use bait
No use carnada
(No oo-say kar-NAH-dah)

Go to the same spot
Vamos al mismo lugar
(VAH-mohs ahl MEES-moh loo-GAR)

I want to fish for
Quiero pescar para
(key-er-oh pes-kar Pah-rah)

I want to fish near shore
Quiero pescar cerca de la orilla
(Key-er.oh pes-Kar Ser-ka day lah oh-REE-yah)

I want to fish deep
Quiero pescar mas hondo
(Key-er-oh pes-Kar maas OHN-doh)

What kind of fish is that?
¿Qué clase de pescado es?
(Kay KLAH-say day pes-KAH-doh es)

Bring in the line
Enrolla la línea
(En-ROLL-yah lah LEEN-eyah)

Stop! I want to cast.
¡Alto! ¡Quiero castear!
(ALL-toh! Key-ere-oh kahs-tay-ARE)

Gaff it
Enganchalo
(En-GAHN-cha-loh)

Let's go
Vamonos
(VAH-moh-nos)

How much do I owe you?
¿Cuanto le debo?
(KWAHN-toh lay DAY-boh?)

Is there? Are there?
There is. There are.
¿Hay? Hay
(eye)

I have
Tengo
(TEN-go)

Basic Sentences

How does one say …in Spanish?
¿Como se dice …en Español?
(KO-mo say DEE-say en es-pahn-YOL)
Either point to the object in question or insert the English word.

Speak slowly, please.
Hable despacio, por favor.
(AH-blay deh-SPA-cee-oh, por-fah-VOR)

Can you help me?
¿Puede usted ayudarme?
(poo-EH-de OO-sted ah-you-DAR-may)

What is your name?
¿Como se llama?
(KOH-moh say YAH-mah)

My name is …
Mi nombre es …
(Me NOM-bray ess)

I want
Quiero
(Key-ER-oh)

I need
Necesito
(neh-ceh-SEE-toh)

I'm hungry
Tengo hambre
(TEN-goh ahm-bray)

I'm thirsty
Tengo sed
(TEN-goh sehd)

Gamefish

Albacore
Ahi-bah-KOH-ra

Amberjack
Pez FUER-tay

Barracuda
Bah-rah-KOO-dah

Bonito
Bar-e-LET-tay

Cabrilla
Cah-BREE-yah

Corvina
Cor-VEE-nah

Dorado
Doh-RAH-doh

Halibut
Lehn-GWAH-doh

Ladyfish
Sab-A-lo

Grouper
Gah-ro-pa

Jack Crevalle
TOR-o

Jewfish
MER-o

Mackerel
Mah-kah-re-li-ah

Marlin
MAHR-leen

Mullet
LEE-sah

Needlefish
Mar-see-AHL

Pompano
Pah-lo-MAY-tah

Roosterfish
Pehs-GAH-yoh

Sailfish
Pez veh-la

Sardines
Sahr-DEE-nahs

Shark
Tee-boo-ROAN

Sierra
see-air-ah

Snapper
PAR-go

Snook
Roh-BAH-lo

Wahoo
Wa-hoo

Tuna
A-tun

Yellowtail
Who-REL

Southern Baja Fly Fishing Resources

Tackle, Charters and Guides
Vista Sea Sport Dive Masters
http://www.vistaseasport.com/
011-52-624-141-0031
vseasport@aol.com

David Jones
http://www.fishermensfleet.com/
011-52-612-1221313 or fax 011-52-612-1257334
david@fishermensfleet.com

Baja Anglers
http://www.baja-anglers.com/
Marina 8-6 Darsena
Cabo San Lucas, Baja California Sur, Mexico
Phone from anywhere in the U.S.
011-52-624-143-4995
banglers@cabonet.net.mx

East Cape Tackle
http://bajadestinations.com/
directory/eastcapetackle/
eastcapetackle.htm
Phone/Fax 011-52-114-10366
hookup@eastcapetackle.com

Minerva's Baja Tackle
http://www.minervas.com/
Apartado Postal 156
Cabo San Lucas, B.C.S. Mexico
Tel: 011-52-624-143-1282
Fax: 011-52-624-143-0440
minerva@minervas.com

Cortez Yacht Charters
http://www.cortezcharters.com/
3609 Hartzel Drive Spring Valley, Ca 91977
Phone: (619) 469-4255
Fax: (619) 461-9303
cortezcharters@sbcglobal.net

The Baja Big Fish Company
http://www.bajabigfish.com/
APDO #200
Loreto, B.C.S. 23880
011-52-613-104-0781

Baja on the Fly
http://www.bajafly.com/
PO Box 300189
Escondido Ca 92030
(800) 919-2252
(760) 746-7260
bajafly@bajafly.com

U.S. Fly Tackle
San Diego Fly Shop
http://www.sandiegoflyshop.com/
124 Lomas Santa Fe Drive #208
Solana Beach, CA 92075
(858) 350-3111

Stroud Tackle
http://www.stroudtackle.com/
1457 Morena Blvd.
San Diego Ca 92130
(619) 276-4822

Andy Montana's Surfside
Fly Fishers
http://www.andymontanas.com
957 Orange Avenue
Coronado, Ca 92118
(619) 435-9993

Bob Marriott's Fly Fishing Store
http://www.bobmarriotts.com/
2700 W. Orangethorpe
Fullerton, Ca 92833
(800) 535-6633
bmfsinfo@bobmarriotts.com

Orvis Company Store
San Francisco
http://www.orvis.com/
intro.asp?subject=625
248 Sutter Street
San Francisco, CA US, 94108
(415) 392-1600

Keine's Fly Shop
2654 Marconi Ave
Sacramento, Ca
(800) 4000-FLY
(916) 486-9958
http://www.kiene.com/
info@kiene.com

Reno Fly Shop
http://www.renoflyshop.com/
Located in Independence Square
in Southwest Reno
294 East Moana Lane, #14
Reno, Nevada 89502
(775) 825-FISH
info@renoflyshop.com

J.D.'s Big Game Fishing Tackle
http://www.jdsbiggame.com
406 South Bayfront
Balboa Island, CA 92662
(949) 723-0883
(800) 660-5030
(949) 723-0810
jdsbiggame@aol.com

Baja on the Internet
Gene Kira's Baja Destinations
http://bajadestinations.com/

Baja Links
http://www.bajalinks.com

Gringo Gazette
http://www.gringogazette.com

Try Baja
http://www.trybaja.com

Mexico On Line
http://www.mexonline.com

Baja Life
http://www.bajalife.com

Baja Nomad
http://www.bajanomad.com

Baja Maps
http://www.baja.com/maproom/
b98/

Baja Weather
Baja Weather Net
http://www.baja-cabo.com/
weather/bwn.html

Tropical Storms
http://www.intellicast.com/

Southern Baja Fly Fishing Resources

Mexico Satellite Photo
http://www.weather.com/maps/
maptype/satelliteworld/
mexicosatellite_large.html

Fly Fishing
Federation of Fly Fishers
http://www.fedflyfishers.org/
(406) 585-7592

International Game Fish Associaton
http://www.igfa.org/
300 Gulf Stream Way
Dania Beach, FL 33004
(954) 927-2628
igfahq@aol.com

Recommended Reading
The Baja Catch by Gene Kira
http://bajadestinations.com/books/
tbc3/tbc3.htm

King of the Moon by Gene Kira
http://bajadestinations.com/books/
kom/kom.htm

Unforgettable Sea of Cortez
by Gene Kira
http://bajadestinations.com/books/
ufsc/ufsc.htm

Baja on the Fly by Nick Curcione
http://www.amazon.com/exec/
obidos/ASIN/1571881018/
bajaonthefly/102-3612332-
2412159

Mexico Blue-Ribbon Fly Fishing
Guide by Ken Hanley
http://www.amazon.com/exec/
obidos/ASIN/1571881549/
bajaonthefly/102-3612332-
2412159

The Magnificent Peninsula
http://www.amazon.com/exec/
obidos/ASIN/1891275038/
bajaonthefly/102-3612332-
2412159

California Fly Fisher Magazine

Other Guidebooks
http://www.amazon.com/

http://www.bookzone.com/

http://www.powells.com/

http://atb.away.com/index.html

http://www.barnesandnoble.com

http://www.flyfishingbooks.us/

Air Travel
Continental Airlines
http://www.continental.com/
Default.asp

Delta Airlines
http://www.delta.com/

United Airlines
http://www.united.com/

Travel Agents
Lynn Rose Tours
http://www.lynnrosetours.com/
(800) 525-9527

Cass Tours
http://www.casstours.com/
(800) 593-6510

Government Resources

Secretary of Tourism
http://www.bajacalifornia.gob.mx/
english/home.htm

U.S. State Department
http://travel.state.gov/
travel_pubs.html

Mexico Consular
Information Sheet
http://travel.state.gov/mexico.html

Travel Clubs
Vagabundos Del Mar
Boat and Travel Club
http://www.vagabundos.com/
contact.htm
190 Main Street
Rio Vista, CA 94571
(800) 474-BAJA (2252)
(707) 374-5511
info@vagabundos.com

Discover Baja
http://www.discoverbaja.com/
index.htm
3089 Clairemont Drive
San Diego, California 92117
(619) 275-4225
(800) 727-BAJA (2252)
Fax: (619) 275-1836
ask@discoverbaja.com

Fly Fishing The Internet
http://www.flyshop.com
http://www.fbn-flyfish.com
http://www.flyfishamerica.com
http://www.gofishing.com/
http://www.fly-fishing-
women.com
http://www.tu.org/index.asp
http://www.flyfishing.com
http://www.2hwy.com/mx/
homepage.htm
http://www.amrivers.org
http://gorp.away.com/index.html
http://www.flyfish.com

Knots
http://members.aol.com/
idfrank/knots.html
http://www.fishingcairns.com.au/
page6-1.html
http://www.rodworks.on.ca/
knotbk.html

No Nonsense Knot Tying Guide

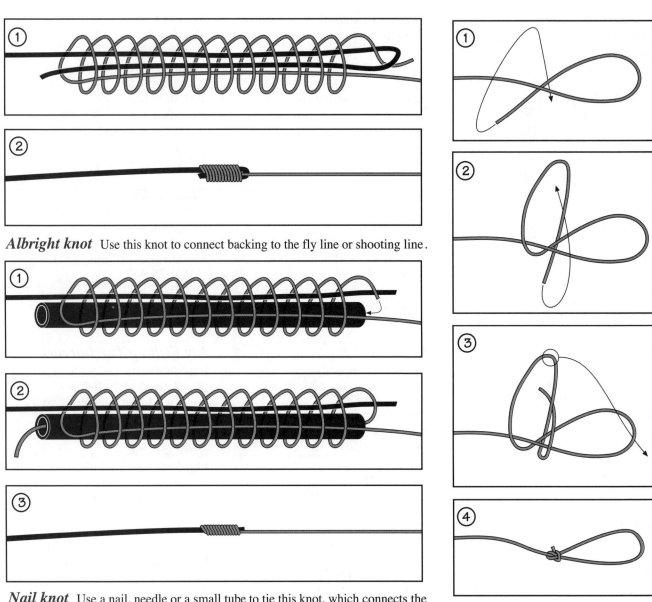

Albright knot Use this knot to connect backing to the fly line or shooting line.

Nail knot Use a nail, needle or a small tube to tie this knot, which connects the forward end of the fly line to the butt end of the leader. Follow this with a Perfection Loop, and you've got a permanent end loop that allows easy leader changes.

Perfection Loop Use this knot to create a loop in the butt end of the leader.

Arbor knot Use this knot to attach your backing to your fly reel. Saltwater fly fishing requires frequent backing changes. Be sure to carry plenty of extra backing!

Loop To Loop Use this simple knot to connect the leader to an end loop on the tip of the fly line.

No Nonsense Knot Tying Guide

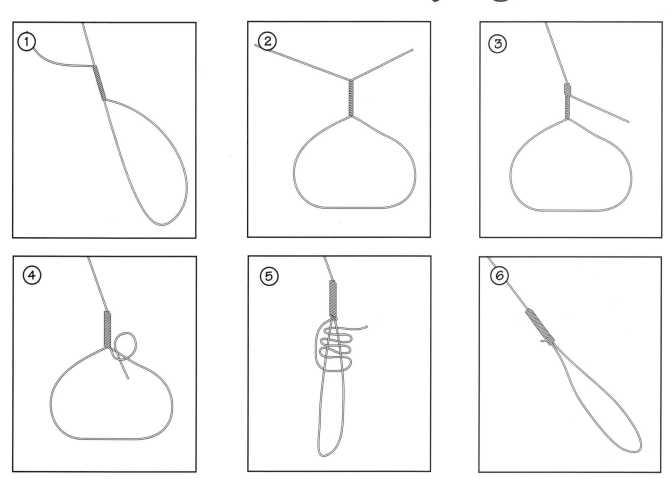

Bimini Twist Very important knot for building shock-absorbing leaders, and very difficult to tie. Nearly 100% knot strength. **1.** Form loop and twist 20 times. **2.** Slip the loop over your knee and pull ends apart, forcing the twists together. **3.** Pull tag end at a right angle to the column of twists while pulling up on the standing end. Pull slightly downward on tag end and allow it to wrap around the column toward the loop. **4.** Continue to roll tag end around the column of twists until you reach the loop. Pinch the last wrap between fingers and make a half-hitch around one leg of the loop and pull tight. Remove loop from knee. **5.** Grab tag end and make 4 or 5 turns over both legs of the loop, wrapping backward toward the base of the loop. **6.** Pull and tighten slowly, causing the spirals to bunch up against base of loop. Trim tag end.

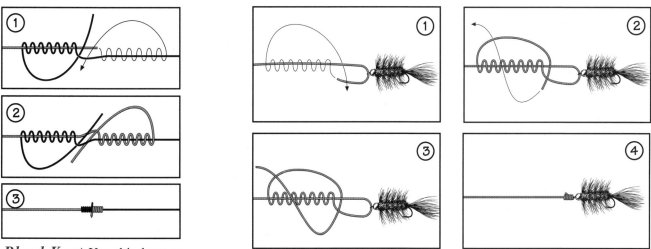

Blood Knot Use this knot to connect sections of leader material. To add a dropper, leave the heavier tag end long and attach fly.

Improved Clinch Knot Use this knot to attach a fly to the end of the tippet.

Fly Fishing Terms for Southern Baja

Especially for the Beginner

Action
Describes the relative resistance to bending as you move down the length of a particular fly rod.

Anti-Reverse Reel
Reel handle does not spin when line is pulled from reel.

ATV
Four-wheel motor bikes used on the beach.

Back Cast
When casting, the propelling of the line behind you.

Backing
The first line loaded on the reel before the fly line.

Barbless
A hook that has the barb pinched down for safety.

Beadhead
A style of fly that incorporates a metal bead near the eye of the hook for weight.

Bimini Twist
A knot that creates a loop with shock absorption.

Bite Tippet
A 12" section of heavier line used at the end of the class tippet to prevent a fish with teeth or a bill from breaking the line.

Butt Section
The short section of line attached to the fly line before the tippet/leader.

Catch and Release
The practice of releasing a fish so it can fight another day.

Class Tippet
The portion (minimum of 15") of a fly line system that is the weakest link used. When fishing for IGFA records, this portion of line determines the qualifying class. Measured in pounds breaking strength.

Clouser
A fly with weighted eyes which allows it to sink quicker and swim with the hook point up.

Cruiser
Larger boat with cabin, bait tank and head. Usually has a flying bridge.

Direct Drive Reel
The handle spins when line is removed from the reel.

Disk Drag
The system in a reel that allows the angler to control the amount of pressure applied to the fish.

Double Haul
A casting technique with a pulling in and releasing of line during both backcast and forward cast.

False Cast
Extending the amount of line to be cast prior to actual cast.

Floating Line
A fly line that is designed not to sink.

Flying Bridge
An elevated platform on a cruiser from which the Captain drives the boat for better visibility.

Forward Cast
The part of the cast when the line is in front of you.

Full Fly Line
Line with continuous shooting head and running line.

Head
Restroom.

I.G.F.A.
International Game Fish Association. Keeper of worldwide fishing records.

Improved Clinch Knot
A knot used to tie a fly to the end of a leader or a tippet.

Intermediate Fly Line
A fly line that is designed to sink at a controlled rate.

Leader
Monofilament or fluorocarbon line attached to the butt section that forms the class tippet.

Line Class
The breaking strength of the class tippet or leader.

Loading
The act of bending a fly rod at the end of a back cast with the weight of the fly line that's transferred into stored energy held in the fly rod.

Loop to Loop
Knot system that allows quick line changes.

Palming
Using the palm of the hand to apply additional drag or pressure on the reel.

Panga
An open skiff with or without a bait tank.

Polarized Sun Glasses
Specially tinted glasses that reduce glare and allow you to see into the water and get protection from UV rays and hooks. Use amber or yellow in low light, gray in strong light.

Popper
A surface fly that attracts fish with commotion.

Shooting Head
The weighted, forward section of the fly line which casts farther.

Shooting Head System
Fly line with the shooting head and running line attached with a knot. Not a continuous system or full fly line.

Sink Tip
A shorter, weighted portion of line used with a floating line that permits the tip to sink deeper.

Streamer
A fly usually representing baitfish and designed to fish sub-surface.

Stripping Basket
A container worn at the waist to manage the fly line and keep it from tangling.

Super Panga
A deluxe open skiff with center console, bait tank and head.

Tippet
The leader portion and weakest link of a fly line system. Measured in pounds breaking strength. The portion of line that determines the qualifying class.

Weight Forward
Fly line with the weight at the forward part of the line to assist with distance and casting into the wind.

Bill Mason
Bill Mason's No Nonsense Guide
To Fly Fishing In Idaho
The Henry's Fork, Salmon, Snake and Silver Creek plus 24 other waters.

Mr. Mason penned the first fly fishing guidebook to Idaho in 1994. It was updated in 1996 and showcases Bill's 30 plus years of Idaho fly fishing experience.

Bill helped build a major outfitting operation at the Henry's Fork and helped open the first fly shop in Boise. In Sun Valley he developed the first fly fishing school and guiding program at Snug Fly Fishing. Bill eventually purchased the shop, renaming it Bill Mason Sun Valley Outfitters.

Fly Fishing Colorado
Jackson Streit
The Colorado, Rio Grande, Platte, Gunnison, Mountain lakes and more.

Mr. Streit fly fished Colorado for over 28 years and condensed this experience into a guidebook, first published in 1995 and updated, improved and reprinted in 2004.

Jackson started the first guide service in the Breckenridge area and in 1985 he opened the region's first fly shop, The Mountain Angler, which he owns and manages.

Ken Hanley
Ken Hanley's No Nonsense Guide
To Fly Fishing In Northern California
The "Sac", Hat Creek, Russian, reservoirs, saltwater and bass on a fly.

Mr. Hanley has fished all the waters in this guide. While traveling the world and leading adventure expeditions he's caught over 50 species of gamefish. He's also written much on the subject including four other books. Ken also writes outdoor related pieces for a variety of publications.

Terry Barron
Terry Barron's No Nonsense Guide
To Fly Fishing Pyramid Lake
The *Gem of the Desert* is full of huge Lahontan Cutthroat trout.

Mr. Barron is the Reno-area and Pyramid Lake fly fishing guru. He helped establish the Truckee River Fly Fishers Club and ties and works for the Reno Fly Shop.

Terry has recorded the pertinent information to fly fish the most outstanding trophy cutthroat fishery in the U.S. Where else can you get tired of catching 18-25" trout?

Harry Teel
Harry Teel's No Nonsense Guide
To Fly Fishing in Central & Southeastern Oregon
The Metolius, Deschutes, McKenzie, Owyhee, John Day and 35 other waters.
Detailed maps drawn by the author.

Mr. Teel combined his 60 years of fly fishing into the first *No Nonsense* fly fishing guide. It was published in 1993 and updated, expanded and improved in 1998 by Jeff Perin. Jeff owns and operates the Fly Fisher's Place, the fly shop in Sisters, Oregon originally owned by Mr. Teel.

Taylor Streit
Taylor Streit's No Nonsense Guide
To Fly Fishing In New Mexico
The San Juan, Cimarron, Gila, Chama, Rio Grand, mountain lakes and more.

The first all inclusive guide to the top fly fishing waters in the *Land of Enchantment*. Since 1970 Mr. Streit has been *THE* New Mexico fly fishing authority and #1 professional guide. He's also developed many fly patterns used throughout the region. Taylor owned the Taos Fly Shop for ten years and managed a bone fishing lodge in the Bahamas. He makes winter fly fishing pilgrimages to Argentina where he escorts fly fishers and explores.

Dave Stanley
Dave Stanley's No Nonsense Guide
To Fly Fishing In Nevada
The Truckee, Walker, Carson, Eagle, Davis, Ruby, mountain lakes and more.

Mr. Stanley is recognized nationwide as the most knowledgeable fly fisher and outdoorsman in the state of Nevada. He also travels throughout the west and other warm climes where he leads fly fishing excursions. He own's and operates the Reno Fly Shop and a satellite shop in Truckee, California.

The guide's talented coauthor, **Jeff Cavender**, is a Nevada native and manager of the Reno Fly Shop. Jeff teaches fly casting and tying. He's taught and guided all over Nevada and California during the past 30 + years.

Where No Nonsense Guides Come From

No Nonsense guidebooks give a quick, clear, understanding of the essential information needed to fly fish a region's most outstanding waters. The authors are highly experienced and qualified local fly fishers. Maps are tidy versions of the authors sketches.

All who produce No Nonsense guides believe in providing top quality products at a reasonable price. We also believe all information should be verified. We never hesitate to go out, fly rod in hand, to verify the facts and figures that appear in the pages of these guides. The staff is committed to this research. It's dirty work, but we're glad to do it for you.

The illustrations and maps in these books are the work of Pete Chadwell. As a fly fisherman, Pete is more than happy to apply his considerable drawing talents to things that live and float in and on water. His detailed maps are a testimony to his desire for accuracy and to get out and fly fish new waters.

Look for new No Nonsense Fly Fishing guides to other important regions!

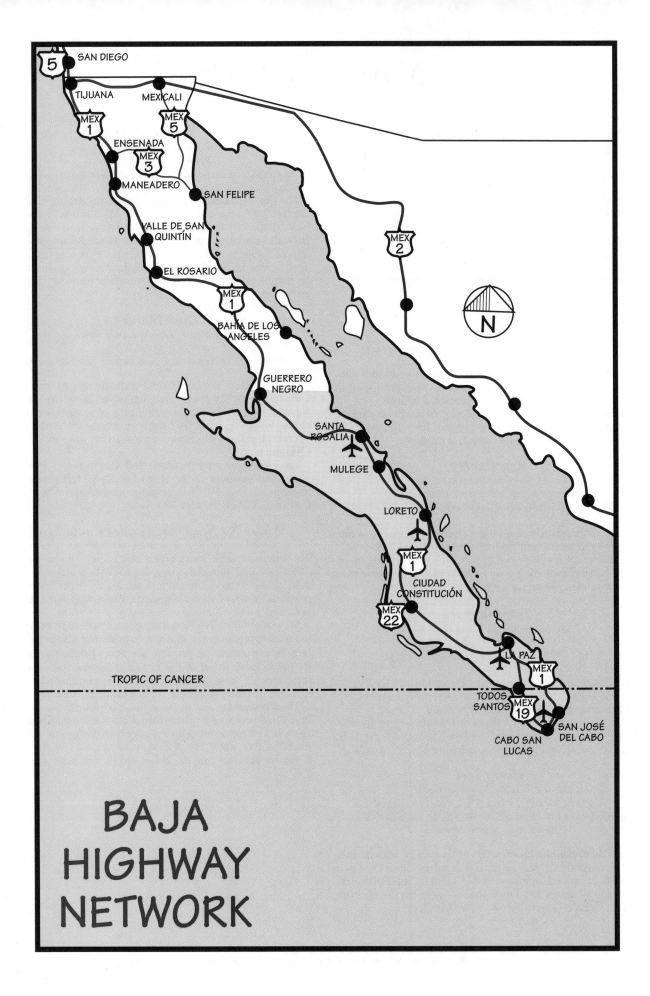

BAJA
HIGHWAY
NETWORK